OAB

Office of Architecture in Barcelona

ACTAR

taxi

OAB
Office of Architecture in Barcelona

PRESENTACION TRABAJOS
OAB

of Architecture in Barcelon

Revisiting the Barcelona Botanical Garden

1989–1999–2009

Carlos Ferrater

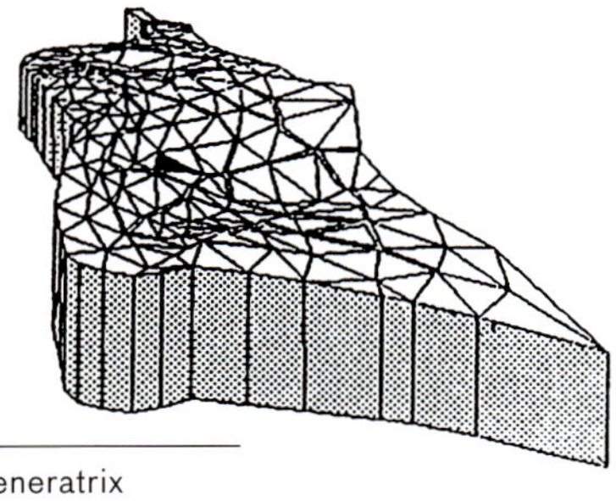

Generatrix

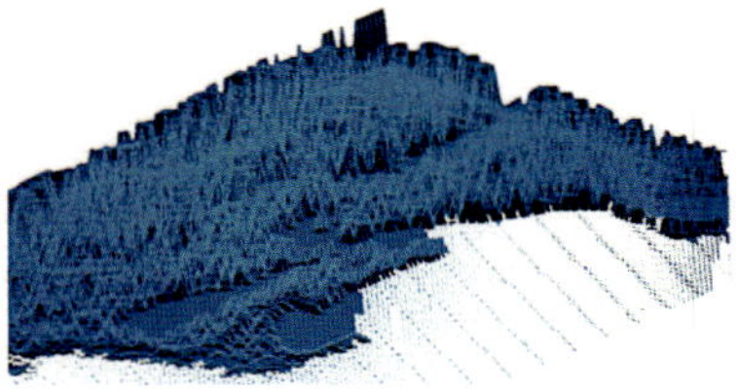

Vertex elevation

Barcelona's Botanical Garden is located on Montjuïc, between the castle and the Lluís Companys Olympic Stadium, on an uneven piece of land and at an altitude between 140 and 100 meters. Its shape is reminiscent of a northwest-facing amphitheater and it has an area of some 14 hectares. For years it has been a municipal waste landfill that has been converted into one of the largest green spaces in the city. It offers magnificent views over the Llobregat delta, the Olympic Ring, and much of the metropolitan area of Barcelona, with the massif of the Garraf and the sierras of Collserola and Marina forming a backdrop.

The most immediate reference is the old Botanical Garden, created by Dr. Pius Font i Quer in the quarries of La Foixarda, Montjuïc, in 1930 and reopened to the public in October 2003. The need to build entrances to the new Olympic facilities in 1986 seriously affected it. This situation helped push forward the proposal to build a new botanical garden in Barcelona, which would house a new building for the Botanical Institute and its collections. Its remit was to be a reference center for the preservation of Mediterranean flora.

The Garden project employs a triangular grid structure fractured by concrete paths that adapt to the terrain and define the routes, the construction and the infrastructure, while at the same time allowing for the harmonious distribution of the units of vegetation. The Garden displays a cross-section of the flora from regions around the world which have a Mediterranean climate. Mediterranean vegetation is considered to be one of the richest in species diversity. It is estimated that only 1.7 percent of the Earth's land surface has a Mediterranean climate, but those same regions account for 20 percent of the world's flora, with more than half being endemic. Today, Mediterranean vegetation is severely threatened, mainly due to human activity. For this reason, the Garden has two main objectives: to contribute to the preservation of plant species and to create a sense of awareness, thereby increasing public respect for nature and the value of biodiversity.

The Mediterranean basin (between latitude 30° and 45° N) is not the only region with a Mediterranean climate. There are other parts of the planet, located at the same latitude in the northern hemisphere or an equivalent latitude in the southern hemisphere, which also have this climate. These areas include south and southwest Australia (between latitude 27° and 37° S), the south of South Africa (between latitude 30° and 35° S), central Chile (between latitude 30° and 37° S), and eastern California (between latitude 30° and 42° N). Together they form the Mediterranean biome, a set of remote plant and animal communities far apart in terms of space but with similar characteristics due to their climatic similarities.

The floral richness of these areas and the similarity of their plants and landscapes are the main source of inspiration for the Barcelona Botanical Garden.

Fractal islands

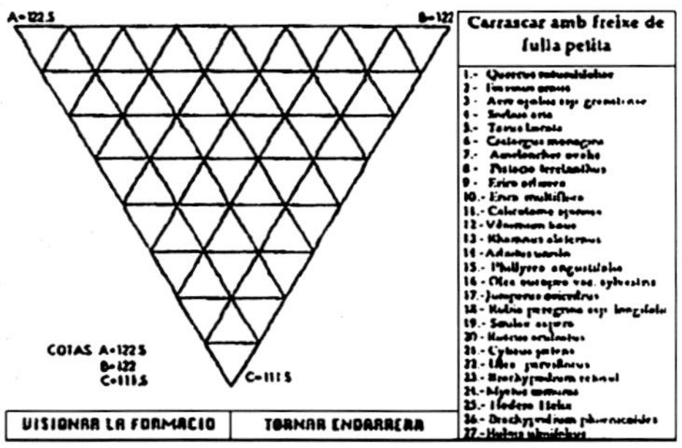

Plant community programme

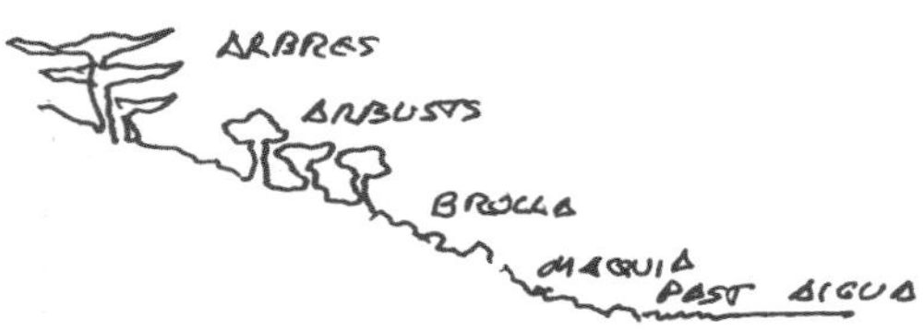

First handmade sketch

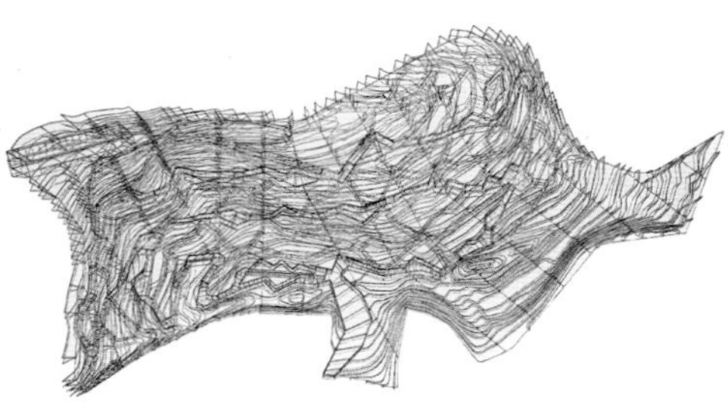

Grid model built in steel fiber

Twenty years have gone by since 1989, when an international design competition to build a new botanical garden on the mountain of Montjuïc was held. The schemes were meant to be developed by interdisciplinary teams consisting of architects, landscape architects, botanists, biologists, engineers, etcetera. Given the failure of unanimous agreement on the part of the jury, the comments by Maria Aurèlia Capmany on the fractal and Mediterranean nature of our proposal worked in our favor and was the deciding factor for the jury to declare us the winner of the competition.

More than ten years have gone by since 1999, the year in which construction of the garden was completed and the first plantings carried out. The first abstract scheme to superimpose a grid on the terrain, to work scale-free, and to incorporate a few tried-and-tested constructional mechanisms, operating on sustainable principles, allowed us to create a new landscape on the original landfill. The current network of paths, walls, and interstitial spaces provides the shape and decoration of the gardens, while the vegetation and plant communities go to form the scientific structure of the garden. The original grid has been visually diminished but still provides the intrinsic natural order of the new landscape. At the end of the intervention, the boundary between the natural and the artificial, structure and ornament, has gradually become undetectable.

In recent years, a series of new additions, further expansion of the network of paths, plantations in the areas of Australia, California and the Mediterranean, as well as new infrastructures such as the multipurpose outdoor space, have completed the earlier intervention.

It is for the above reasons that twenty years after that first competition and ten since the construction of the garden, it is appropriate to revisit and review those founding principles, along with the method for approaching a project and the way of proceeding in constructional terms.

The fractal construction of the landscape

The first consideration was how to arrive at a project design in which the actual site provided the construction guidelines, with emphasis being placed on the morphological and topographical conditions of the new landscape.

The second consideration involved the structure of the new garden, which had to include Mediterranean flora as well as floras from other homoclimatic areas, namely California and a part of Japan in the northern hemisphere and, in the symmetrical zones of the southern hemisphere, parts of Chile, South Africa, and a small region on the Australian coast. The layout of the new garden would be based on botanical and ecosystem values, as well as on the use of the convergent concept of plant morphology, thus becoming a tool of high scientific value and a part of the future of twenty-first-century botanical gardens.

The synthesis of these two aims would only be possible were we to have an instrument capable of promoting dialogue and joint work between the different disciplines, an impossible task in the early days of the project. This is how the idea of a triangular grid on the site emerged. The grid would have to adapt to any unevenness, fraying at the edges, and increases or decreases in the surface according to the varying topographic slope. The guidelines of the triangular grid would follow the three main directions of the contour lines, thus ensuring that two vertices of each triangle were at the same level, datum 0. Other subdivisions of the grid in accordance with the concepts of accessibility, planting, etcetera, would keep to the same structure.

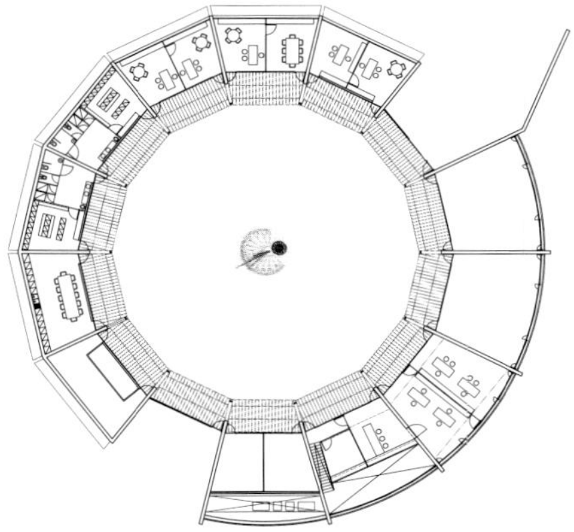

General plan

Botanical Garden Maintenance Building

Under construction March 2015

Watercolour drawing (80 x 65 cm)

Scale topographic model made with different types of wood (50.5 x 70.5 cm)

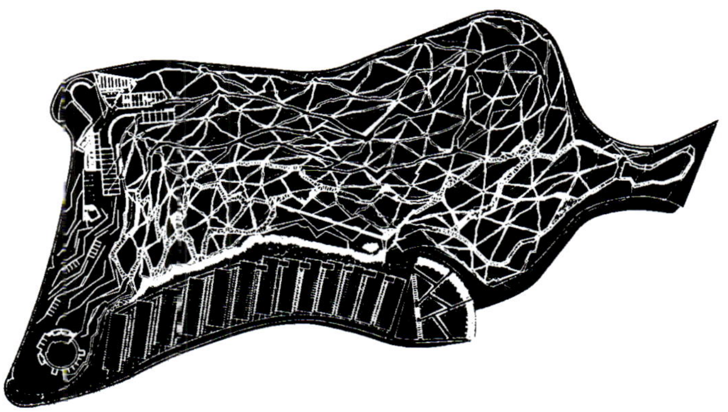

Original grid

The Garden displays different collections of Mediterranean plants distributed according to geographical areas (Australia, Chile, California, South Africa, and the Mediterranean basin), and grouped in turn according to the landscapes they form in nature. These groupings, called phyto-episodes (plant communities), are the exhibition and management units of the Botanical Garden. There are currently 87 phyto-episodes. The forests communities are located in the highest areas and those dominated by shrub-like plants can be found in the central and lower areas.

Australia: the 700,000 km^2 Australian Mediterranean region is the second largest, accounting for just over 20 percent of the biome. It is formed by two separate sectors, located in the southwest and south of the continent. There are some 8,000 known species, 75 percent of which are endemisms. The climate is Mediterranean with some tropical influence due to the proximity of the ocean monsoons, so the summer drought is not as rigorous as in our own Mediterranean area, but even so the frequency of fires is high. In the Australian area of the Garden, in addition to its characteristic Mediterranean flora, warm floras from the southwest of the continent—the states of Victoria and New South Wales—are also cultivated. Both the tree-like and shrub-like plants are dominated by a large number of species from few families, such as the mimosa (*Acacia*), Myrtaceae (*Eucalyptus*, *Melaleuca*, *Callistemon*), and Proteaceae (*Hakea*, *Banksia*, *Grevillea*).

Chile: the Mediterranean area of Chile is a narrow coastal strip of about 100 kilometers corresponding to the region of central Chile. Its area is 140,000 km^2 and it represents less than 5% of the biome. Climatically, it has a rather cool character marked by the influence of the ocean, with plenty of coastal fog. There are some 2,400 known species, 23 percent of which are endemic. An important ecological feature of this area is the historical absence of fire, and a marked presence of herbivores, in particular camelids (llamas and guanacos). There is, therefore, an abundance of thorny bushes and plants are not adapted to fire. The Chilean Mediterranean area has a variety of sclerophyllous landscapes (plants with stiff and rigid leaves), with woodland and shrub formations extending from sclerophyll forest to coastal scrubland, and including *el espinal* or spiny hillside scrublands. Many Chilean plants have the names of Iberian plants as early settlers compared them to those they were familiar with.

California: the Mediterranean area of California occupies a narrow coastal strip from Cape Blanco, in the United States, to Punta Baja, Mexico, with the center more or less in San Francisco. To the east, the strip extends 100–200 kilometers inland. Despite its small size (about 10 percent of the total biome), it is the area with the largest continuous expanses of unchanged Mediterranean landscapes. There are some 4,300 known species, 35 percent of which are endemisms. In climatic terms, seasonality is very pronounced as 85 percent of the rainfall is concentrated in the winter. The summer droughts are very severe but the coastal fog partly relieves this contrast.

South Africa: the South African Mediterranean area is the smallest of all and represents just 3 percent of the biome. There are some 8,550 known species, of which 68 percent are endemic. Rain is most intense in the cold season, although it is never very abundant. Moreover, due to the summer influence of tropical monsoons, there is no completely dry season. Despite the presence of the Mediterranean climate at either end of the African continent, the flora of this region has few genera in common with the Mediterranean basin. The diversity of soils, climate and topography, together with geographical isolation and the recurrence of fires, have led to a high proportion of endemic and rare species, thus making it, along with the southwest of Australia, the most diverse of the Mediterranean areas and one of the richest in the world. In the Garden, the Mediterranean area of The Cape, the subtropical territories of the Karoo and the savannah, and the temperate zones of the southeastern forests are represented.

The Mediterranean Basin: the quintessential Mediterranean area is the Mediterranean Basin, i.e. the lands surrounding the Mediterranean Sea. It stretches across different European, Asian, and African territories and has an area of 2,300,000 km^2. There are some 25,000 known species, of which 50 percent are endemic. Mediterranean flora has many solutions when it comes to adapting to the ecological factors that have influenced its evolution: rigid and persistent leaves to resist the dry summer, spikes, thorns, and toxic substances to defend themselves against herbivores, low plants in the form of a pin cushion, or shrubs that lose their leaves in summer to reduce transpiration. The great capacity for the regeneration of plants in the Mediterranean Basin (five times higher than those of the California chaparral, which is the area it most resembles) clearly shows the importance of centuries of human intervention. Human beings, with the help of ploughs, fire, and cattle, have profoundly shaped Mediterranean plants and landscapes.
The flora of the Mediterranean Basin has been distributed in the Garden in four bio-geographical sub-regions: the eastern Mediterranean (between Italy and the Caucasus), the western Mediterranean (the Iberian Peninsula and Balearic Islands, and the Tyrrhenian Sea), North Africa (from Morocco to Tunisia), and the Canary Islands.

The Barcelona Botanical Institute is located within the Garden. It is a research center with a long tradition in Catalonia, and looks after the main scientific collections created in the country over more than three centuries.
The current building, opened in 2003, includes an exhibition hall open to the public, where people can visit the Cabinet of Natural History.

The Salvador Museum was the first museum to open to the public in Barcelona.

[Text taken from the Col·lecció de Parcs i Jardins of the AMB]

Barcelona Botanical Institute for the Higher Council of Scientific Research

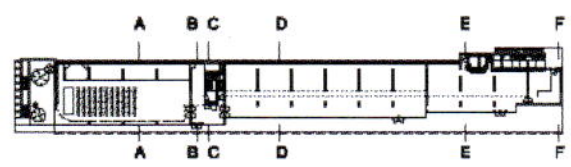

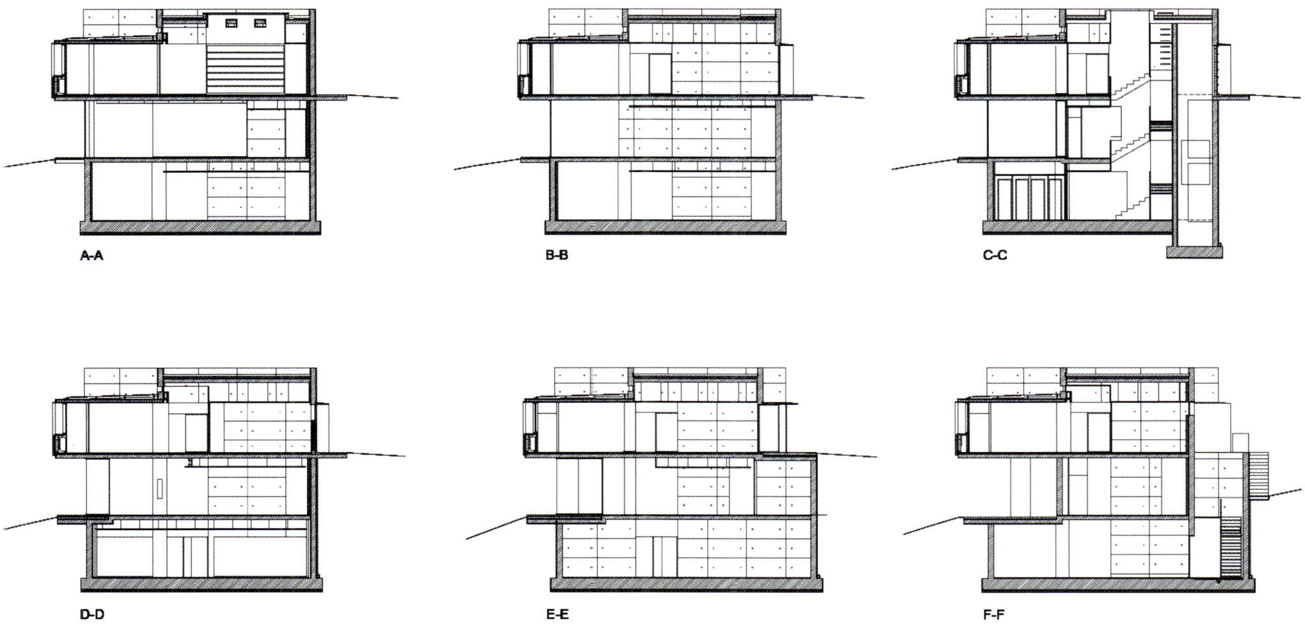

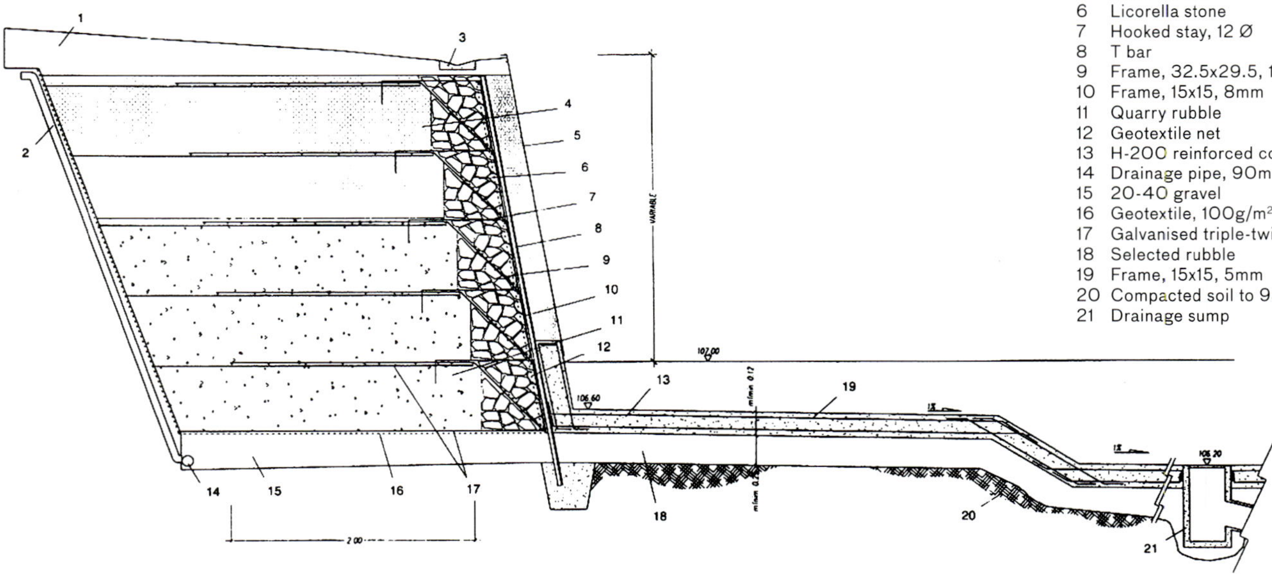

1 Compost
2 Drainage
3 Concrete ditch
4 Selected soil
5 3mm corten
6 Licorella stone
7 Hooked stay, 12 Ø
8 T bar
9 Frame, 32.5x29.5, 10mm
10 Frame, 15x15, 8mm
11 Quarry rubble
12 Geotextile net
13 H-200 reinforced concrete
14 Drainage pipe, 90mm
15 20-40 gravel
16 Geotextile, 100g/m²
17 Galvanised triple-twisted mesh
18 Selected rubble
19 Frame, 15x15, 5mm
20 Compacted soil to 95% avg. porosity
21 Drainage sump

Section of reinforced wall

Residential architecture and the city

Carlos Ferrater

This chapter addresses the issue of multifamily housing, showcasing two buildings simultaneously over time that respond to different typological programs, small apartments in the case of the Vertix Diagonal Building, and larger-scale housing in the M3 Building in Plaa Lesseps. Two spaces undergoing transformation in the city of Barcelona, the first on the recently created Diagonal, and the second in an area that has gone through many changes in recent times.

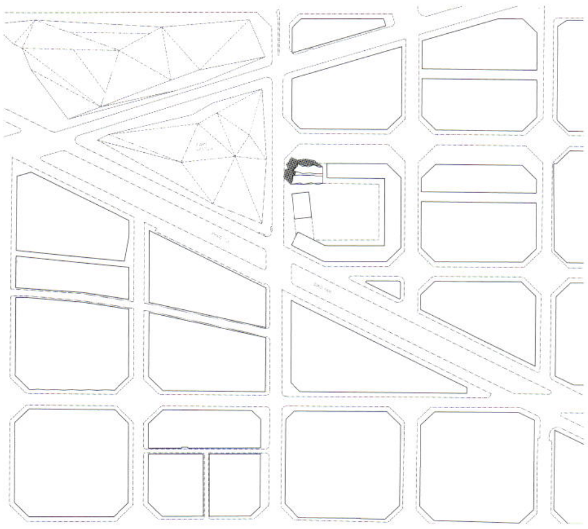

Vertix Diagonal building

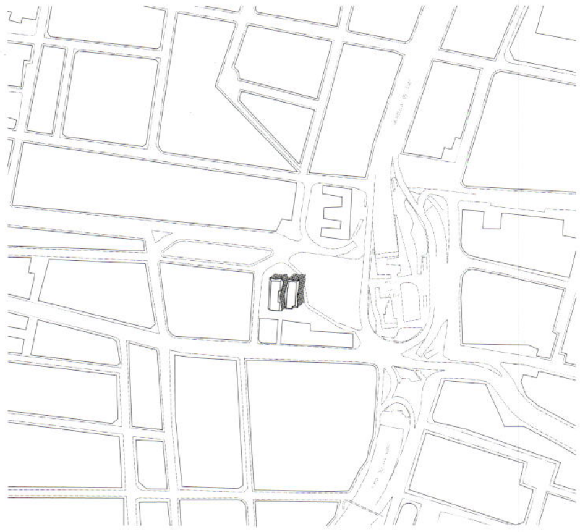

M3 Lesseps building

Both buildings pose questions that deal with the construction of the city, defining urban areas from the architectural project, while raising substantive issues on typological diversity and the construction of flexible and lightweight façades that encompass sustainability, environmental control, and Mediterranean traditions.

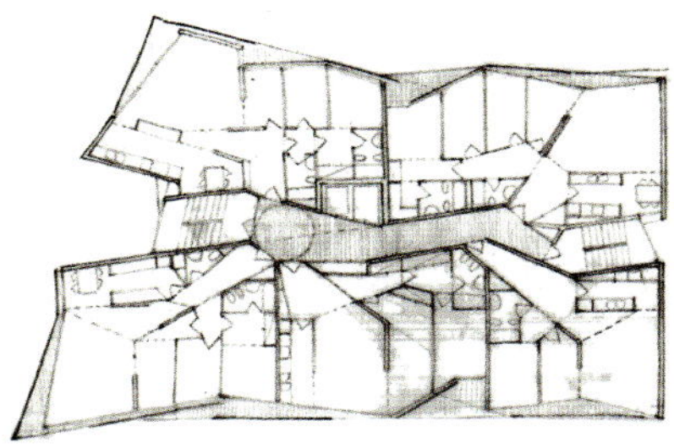

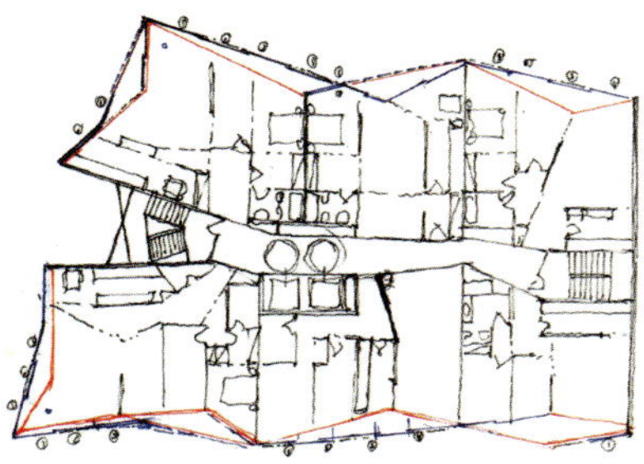

Sketch for Vertix Diagonal building

Carlos Ferrater Xavier Martí Galí

Vertix Diagonal building

On Barcelona's new Diagonal, opposite the Central Park designed by Jean Nouvel at the end of the northern arm of the block, there is a residential building with a twofold purpose: firstly, as the façade of the open block of the Cerdà Plan, and secondly, that of an autonomous entity.

Six apartments per floor are organized around a zigzagging corridor that links the two vertical circulation cores and configures the communal space and light towards the exterior. The houses have intermediate spaces that are arrived at on the basis of the different winding levels of the façade, where the sliding blinds are arranged on both the interior and the exterior. This maintains privacy and light control, yet at the same time helps create open spaces to link inside and outside, making the separation walls of the homes unnecessary.

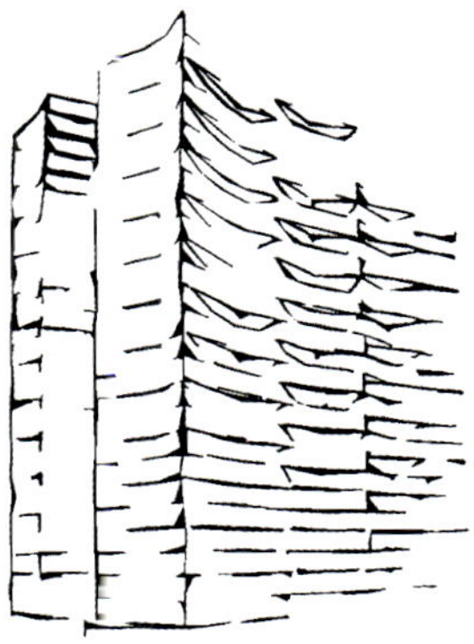

The configuration of the building allows for a variety of typologies. This versatility is reflected in the development of one-, two-, and three-bedroom apartments on the one floor. The dimensions are defined by the treatment of the outer skin. Black-painted steel ribs form the skin of the building, while solving the intertwined form of the metal slats and interior glass around the perimeter of the façade. Fractures in the skin are found in the spaces housing stairs.

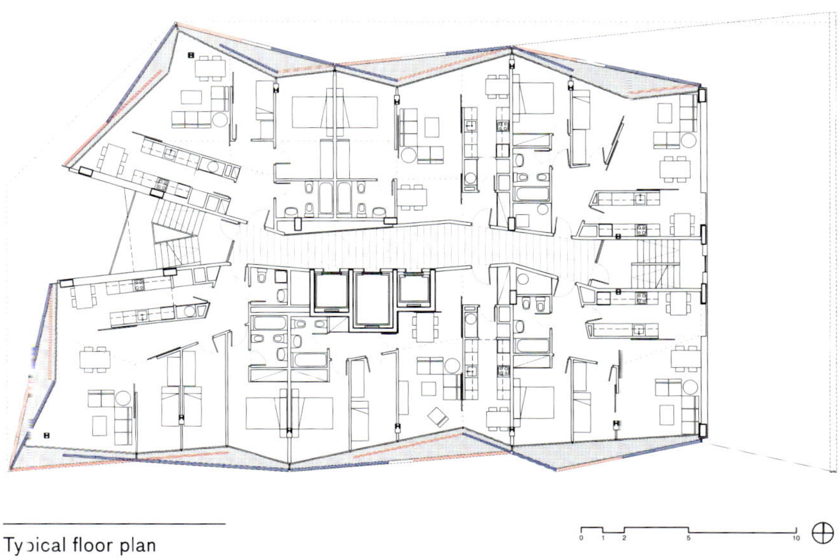

Typical floor plan

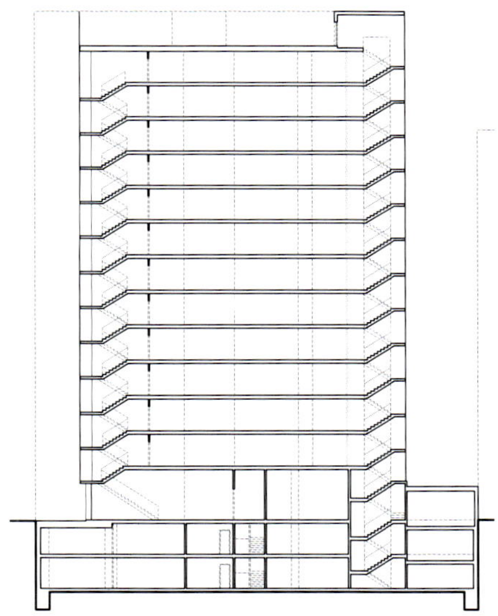

Longitudinal section

The projects presented in this chapter experiment with the intermediate space that is formed at the boundary between the exterior and interior areas of the home. The mobile or fixed shutter elements help to create a place that acts as a climate filter, regulating the degree of privacy and sun control, creating spaces that become an extension of the house, something José Antonio Coderch de Sentmenat experimented with in the houses he built for fishermen in 1955 on Passeig Joan de Borbó, in Barceloneta opposite the port of Barcelona.

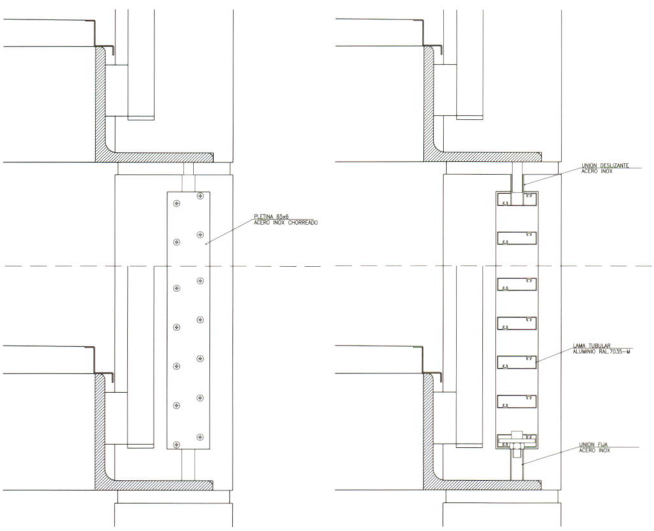

Wall detail

The façades offer a set of fixed and sliding metal shutters that open and close the terraces and allow for better integration of indoor-outdoor spaces, regulating daylight. These shutters, made of stainless steel, transverse tubular crossbeams lacquered in pearl grey. They are framed by fine steel railings forming a grid where the vertical bars create a rhythm and the horizontal beams refine the pace of the framework.

This latticework façade, along with the interior glass planes, wind around the entire perimeter creating interstitial spaces, transition areas between the city and the interior inhabited space, a heritage of Mediterranean architecture.

The building, next to the Joan Fuster library, has been constructed as a symbol of the new Plaça Lesseps in Barcelona.

EN VENDA
PER LLOGAR
T 93 301 77 77

Mobility Infrastructures - Intermodality

Carlos Ferrater

Zaragoza-Delicias Intermodal Station

The international design competition for the Zaragoza-Delicias Intermodal Station, which the Ministry of Development convened among a selection of Spanish and foreign architects including Norman Foster, Santiago Calatrava, Ricardo Bofill, Richard Rogers, Rafael Moneo, and Ábalos & Herreros, allowed us to work in and explore a field that up until a few decades ago was exclusively reserved for the world of transport infrastructure engineering.

The TWA Terminal in New York and the Foster Dulles Terminal in Washington, both designed by Finnish architect Eero Saarinen, were milestones in airport architecture, and in recent times we have witnessed extraordinary airport projects designed by architects such as Norman Foster (Stansted) and Renzo Piano (Kansai Airport).

Working with large flows of people, mobility limitations, and Intermodal connections between different transport modes are all fundamental points:

High-speed trains, buses and coaches, large changeover areas, and parking lots for public and private vehicles demand the effective management of shifting between different modes of transport, making the process more fluid, agiler and faster.

This was one of the challenges posed by the Zaragoza-Delicias Intermodal Rail Station. A city in an indistinct territory, Zaragoza has, with the high-speed train, become an important node 75 minutes away from Barcelona and Madrid—and in the future from Valencia and Bilbao—making it a key station for connections to Europe.

This meant that the design of the station had to allow for quick and efficient connection from all means of transport to the high-speed train. For this reason the station is equipped with double arrival and departure halls, as well as a transfer hall that lies below the tracks—although it has natural light—such that in a few minutes the users of private automobiles, public transport, coaches or trains are able to access the high-speed trains via automatic doors. This layout is similar to the way an airport operates—a typological experiment for new twenty-first-century stations.

Delicias Station is structured as a major nexus of growth in the city, as was the basilica of El Pilar in its day. The station helps to merge two districts. It provides the backbone for the Expo towards the River Ebro, and it has become a nucleus for the services sector and for different facilities, which are located around the large 40,000 m^2 structure (the equivalent of eight football pitches in size). The station has a roof suspended on large arches and a tetrahedron mesh that provides natural light, good acoustics, and a high level of environmental comfort, while retaining the spatiality of the traditional station.

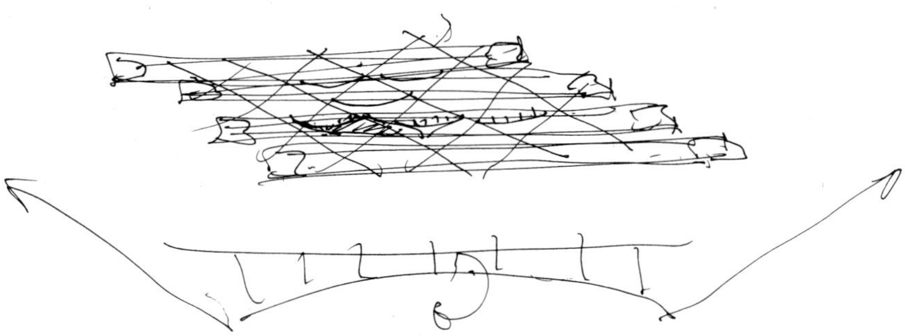

Altaria

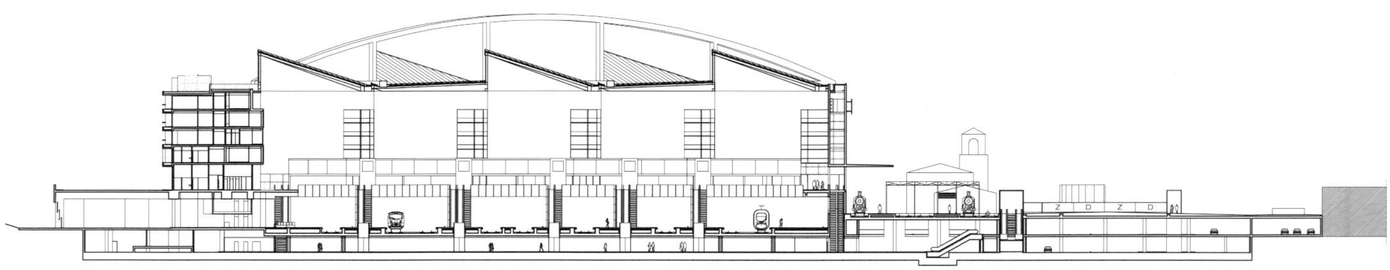

Cross section

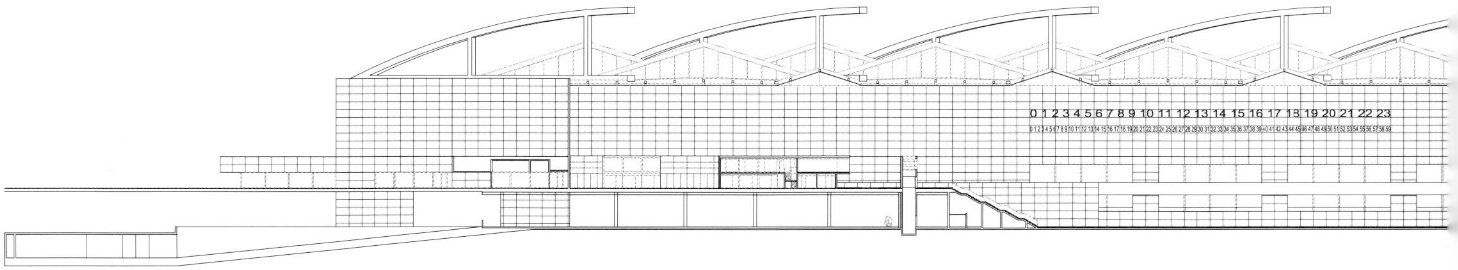

Longitudinal section

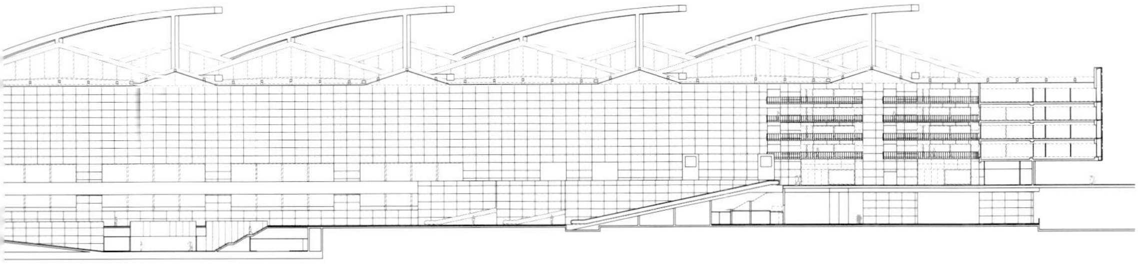

The Intermodal Building at Barcelona Airport

After the experience in Zaragoza, and on being named finalists in the competition for the new terminal at Barcelona Airport, we decided, along with Ramon Sanabria and J.M. Casadevall, to set up a studio to develop projects in the field of transport infrastructure, projects which involved collaborating with different engineers.

This has allowed us to carry out several projects in the airport of Barcelona, such as the multimodal building, which we are currently working on, the façade of the new city airport, and the Metro Line 9 station at Terminals 1 and 2. We are also working on the construction of Murcia Airport, after winning the competition organized by the Ministry of Infrastructure in 2008. However, to date our greatest achievement has perhaps been the Intermodal Building at Barcelona Airport. The design has a neutral, opaque façade consisting of sleek aluminum profiles, while the frieze by Joan Miró puts the finishing touch to the enclosure between the old Terminals A and B.

An independent volume with a glass skin on all four faces, the building provides for the gradual fusion of natural and artificial light by giving this new space a floating and seemingly empty feel, even though it is full of travellers.

Both the train station in Zaragoza, which won the 2004 Brunel Award, and the Intermodal Building for Barcelona Airport, which earned the Flight International Award, raise questions about generic space. A station that becomes a micro indoor city with hotels, restaurants, office buildings, convention centers, shops, and cultural activities, offers a hybrid co-existence between traditional public space and generic space, as advocated by Rem Koolhaas.

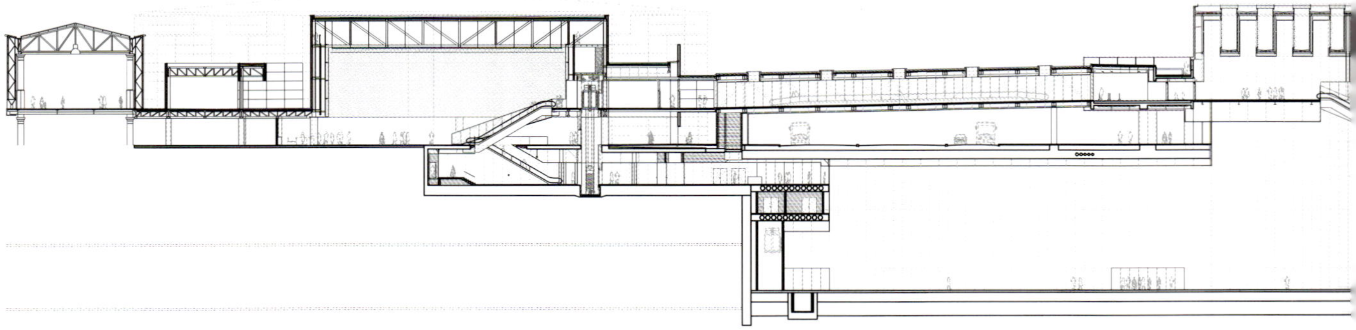

Longitudinal section

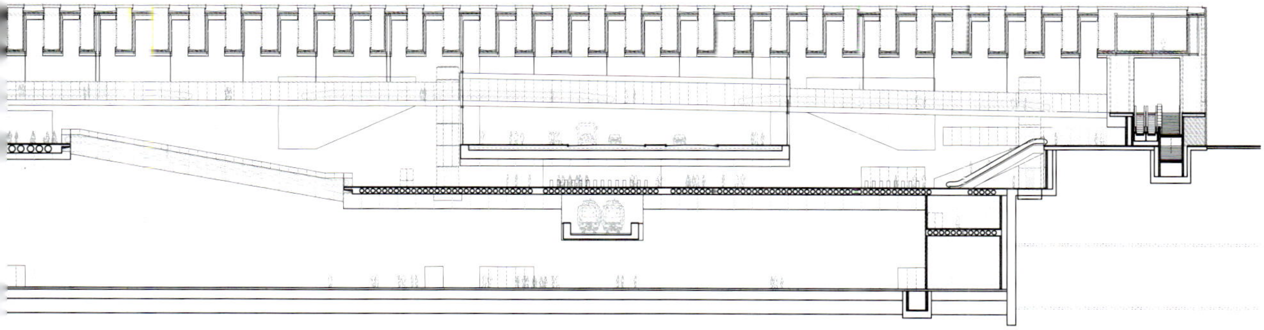

Murcia Airport

The new airport needed to respond rigorously and rationally to the physical, environmental and social conditions of its location, a location closely connected with the Mediterranean, and had to establish an intelligent insertion while providing a clear and pertinent response to the site and its environment.

The program demanded a building with an ongoing capacity for change, since several possible scenarios were proposed, scenarios which would change over time. In fact, we had to confront a building in which change was to be a permanent feature, something that is extremely common in this kind of infrastructure. The building, then, had to respond with utmost clarity to almost certain change, while maintaining its appearance and identity.

An airport is inevitably an access door to a given place. In our case to the region of Murcia, and what is more transmissible that the name itself? Hence, the letters of that name were to become an integral part of the new airport, and would remain linked to its permanence.

Hence, tts main façades, airside and landside, are composed of the word MURCIA. The rest may change, but the identity of the name will be forever associated with its presence and its ties to the setting. It will be the first airport in which the name of the location establishes the entire image of its identity.

The basic materials were aluminum and glass, which give a sense of lightness and permeability. Besides being closely related to the world of aviation, aluminum is a material used in lightweight construction, and may even be associated with an ephemeral type of building. This, and its chameleonic chromatism, are in our opinion the clearest and simplest responses to the location.

Ramon Sanabria & Carlos Ferrater

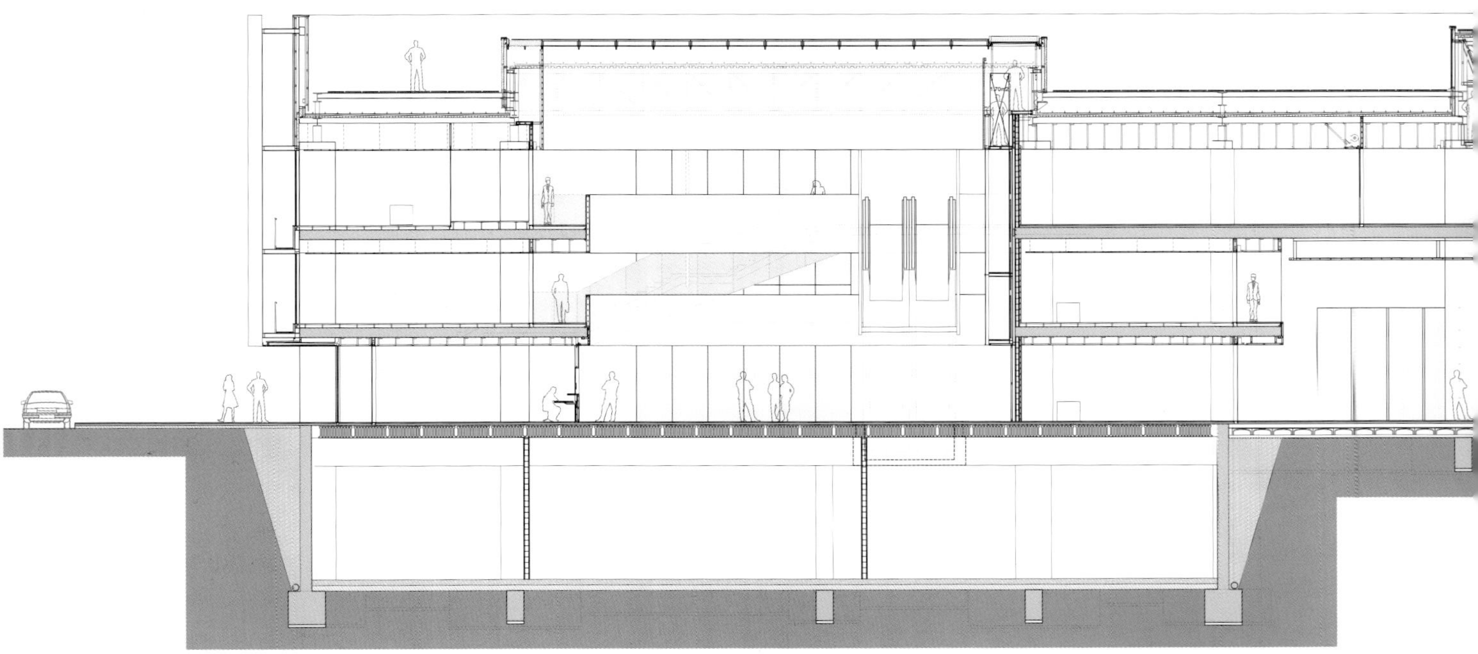

URCIA

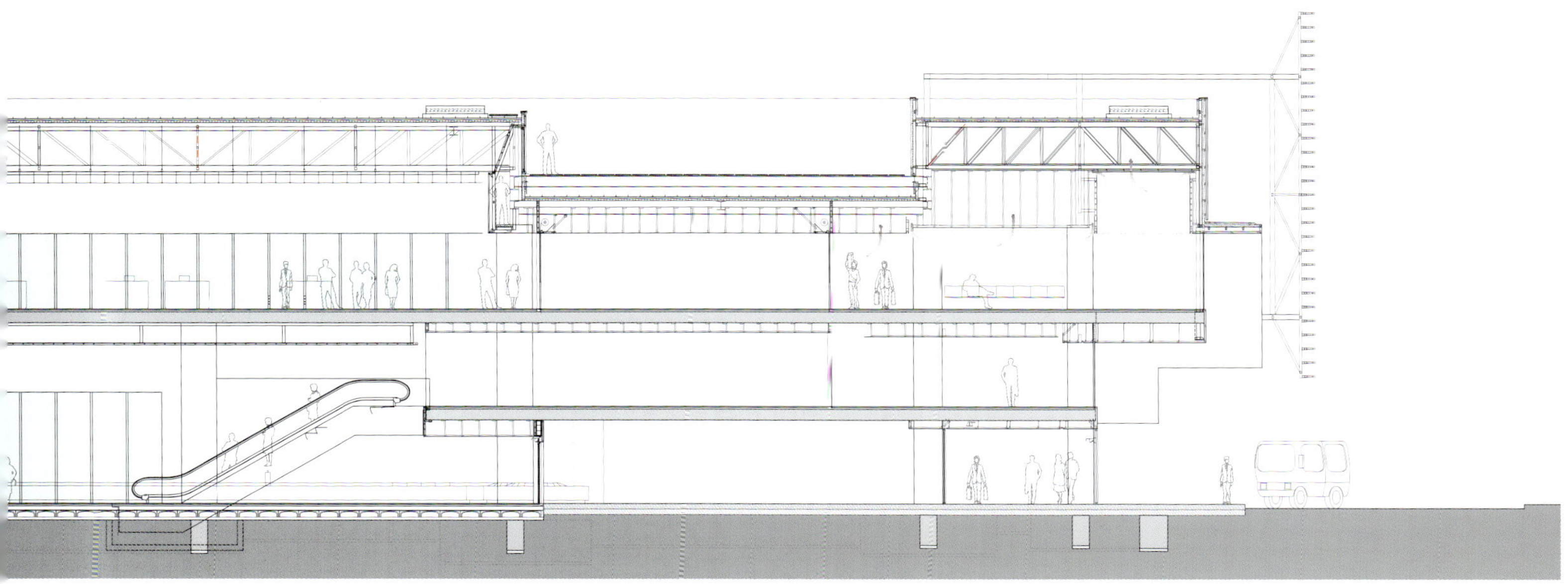

02

Rediscovering the Morphology of the Eixample

Joan Busquets

The development of the Cerdà Eixample has become a laboratory for the evolution of architectural and urban forms.

We might argue that the special contrast between the geometric rigidity of the Cerdà Plan and the complexity of the geographical order of the "Llano de Barcelona"—formed by a system of roads, drainage systems, and properties—resulted in the morphological development of the Eixample, which at first sight seems contradictory, but is perhaps one of the reasons for the great spatial richness and diversity of its built-up, functional system.

It is common knowledge that Cerdà's initial premise of reserving much of the center of the city blocks as communal open spaces was immediately overridden due to the increasing need to use those spaces for industrial plant and major services. This initial scheme has met with a response in more recent interventions, based on the 1985 city ordinance to once again free up the center of the block for landscaped spaces, and in some instances the city block courtyard has been reserved for public use.

Joan Busquets is Professor of Urban Planning Design in Harvard Graduate School of Design

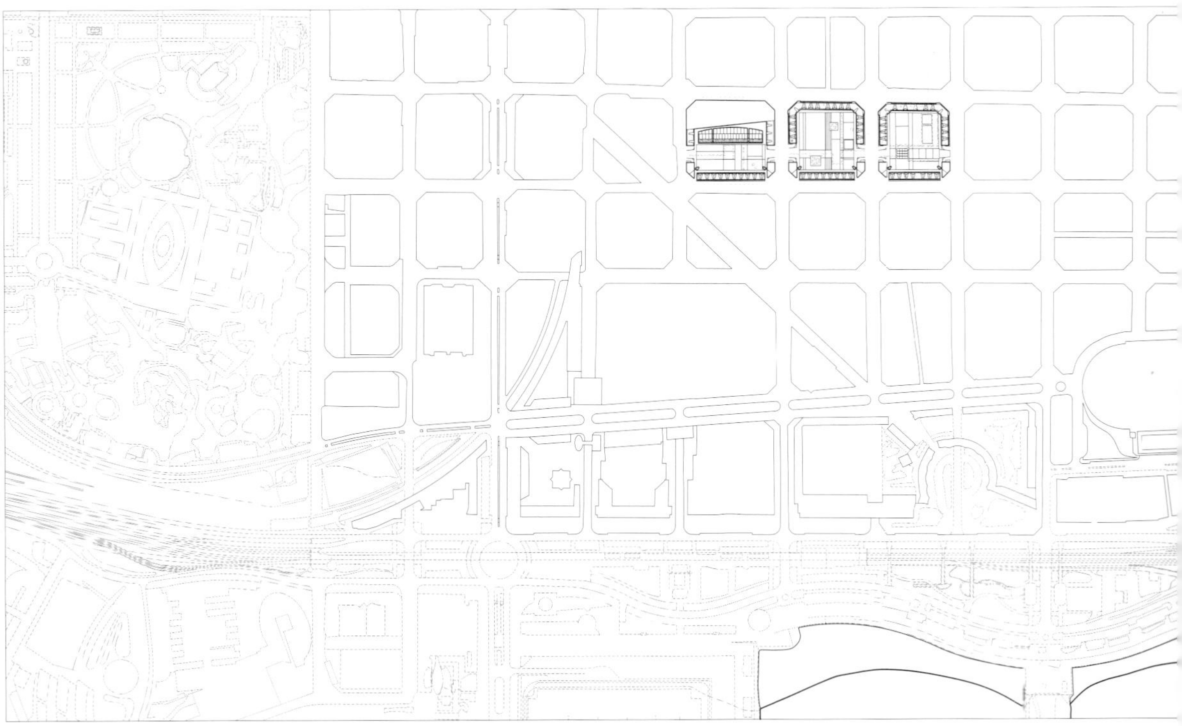

Three blocks in the Eixample, 1992

The development of the Eixample over 150 years or more has led to the consolidation of the closed-block building, concentrated in the skin of the block through the setting up of two well-defined situations: streets and corners. This has led to a fairly consistent system which different generations of architects have inflected with very different programs and stylistic hypotheses. On celebrating the 150th anniversary of the Cerdà Plan in the exhibition at the CCCB, we tried to investigate this hypothesis by mapping relevant examples relative to these two situations: either in a line (that is, by following the street), or on a corner: namely, by resolving the meeting of the perpendicular directions of the streets. Such an exercise gauges the richness of this typological laboratory, the Eixample, in which it is clear that the stylistic conditions are no more than a complement to other crucial factors like the insertion of the functional program, and/or the width of the land lot on which the architecture is developed.

What stands out in this recent research is the set of proposals by Carlos Ferrater and his team in the formation of a host of typological schemes of great interest in both of the situations mentioned above, be they "corner" or "line," and in keeping with the tradition already established by the MBM studio in the 1960s. These efforts are of great value because they are restricted to privately developed interventions and are therefore rarely conducive to research projects involving any risk. Several schemes for buildings in a line and in particular efforts to deconstruct the corner are particularly praiseworthy, as in most cases they are infill operations within the existing grid and therefore subject to the residual logic of some of these plots.

Semi-open blocks with houses inside

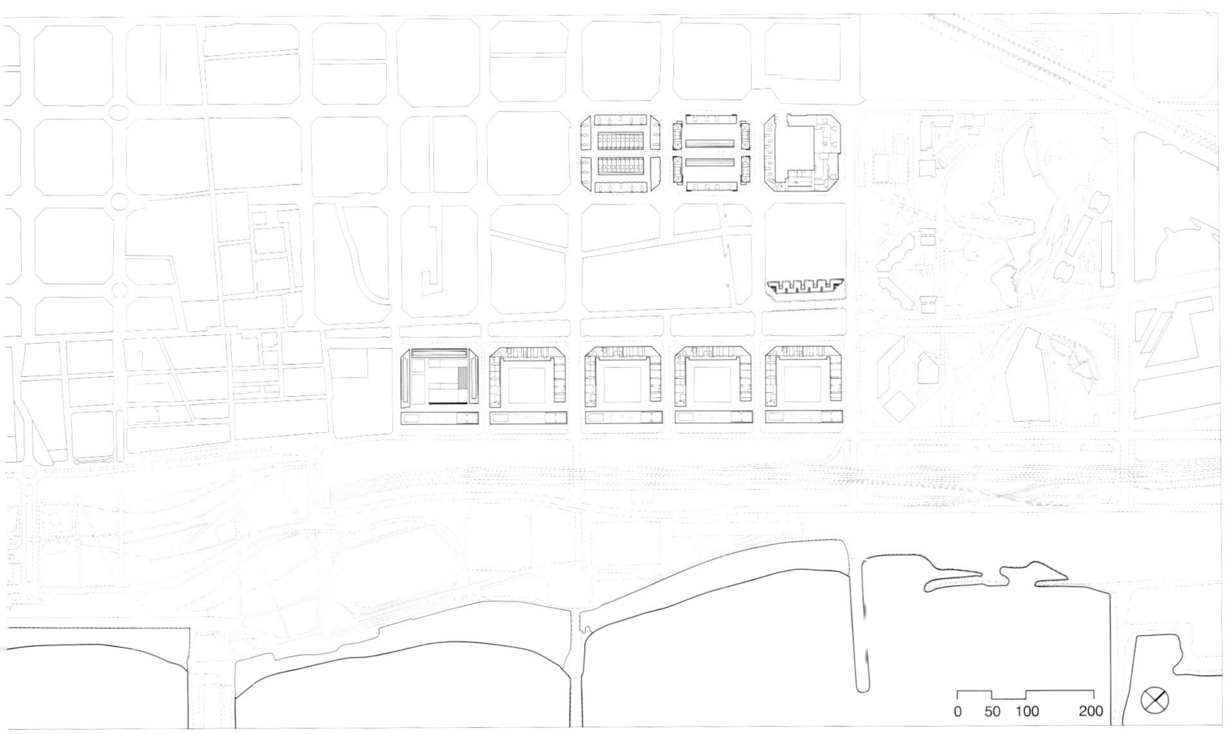

Five blocks in the seafront, 2010

Regesa social housing, 1998

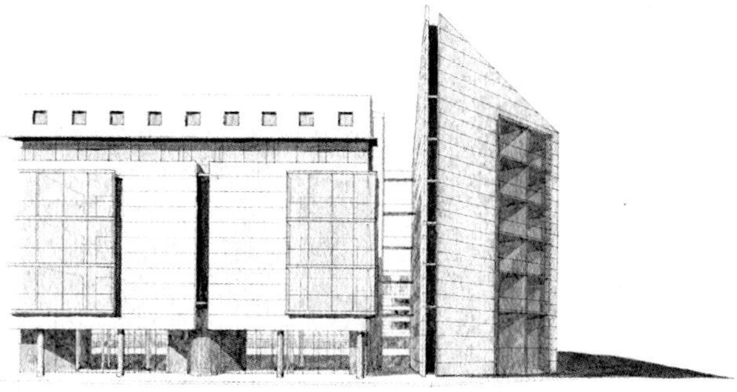

To be sure, the team's reflections on the Eixample are particularly interesting when they have to do with the defining of new morphologies in those projects that offer the possibility of positing the architectural definition of entire blocks. It is here that taking another look at the Cerdà Plan has found a new dimension. In fact, new morphological interpretations are involved in projects like the second Olympic Village in Poble Nou or the "Five Blocks" on the seafront.

In both of these cases the Ferrater team attempts to provide a specific response to the fact that the project might intervene in a land lot larger than that of the architectural plot itself, and may have to confront the logic of the perimetral building and of the interior space of the city block with new options.

The first case seeks to rediscover the city block courtyard as the articulating element of the complex, producing an aggregate of three blocks that can have their own independent use even though they respond to a logic that permits a single reading. To a certain extent they seem, here, to rework the rudiments of those passages which bisect and connect various blocks in the central Eixample. Within this morphological principle, the architecture seeks ways to create singular groups, and the typological research is based on interesting principles of constructional rationality. Meanwhile, in order to resolve the meeting of the corners the exploration relies on privileging the "line" of the building.

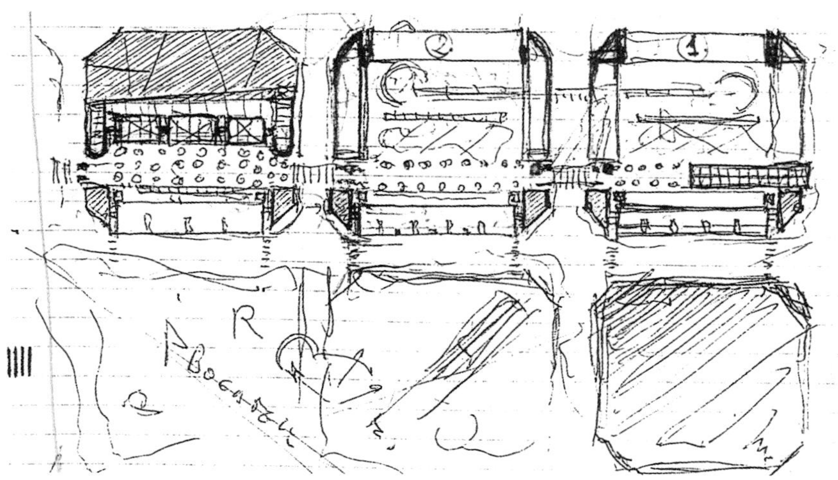

For the “Five Blocks” on the seafront, the research is different. Once again, the idea that the closed block has to permit perception of the inner courtyard is explored but here the gamble lies in singling out one façade of the city block, the seaward one, in order to formulate a composition which goes beyond the individuality of each block and banks on a multi-block composition that plays with main sightlines of the seafront and the possibility that more unique uses might formalize the frontage of these spaces. This exercise seems to introduce the solution of the hybrid block as a way of tackling the problem of the singular points. The greater height of the new corners, which are now frontal entities, allows these buildings to stand out without turning them into individual features at odds with the complex.

We should add that the long periods of testing carried out by the Ferrater team on the Eixample verifies the enormous adaptability of the geometric provisions of the city blocks proposed by Cerdà. It also demonstrates the team’s unwavering commitment to go on innovating and to show how new programs ought to come up with new typological answers. But above all, to concern itself with how the varied deconstruction of a city block can introduce different compositional forms from which special morphological options are designed. Despite the individuality of these options they continue to maintain a high level of consistency with the deployment of the monumental typology of which the Eixample is a historical legacy.

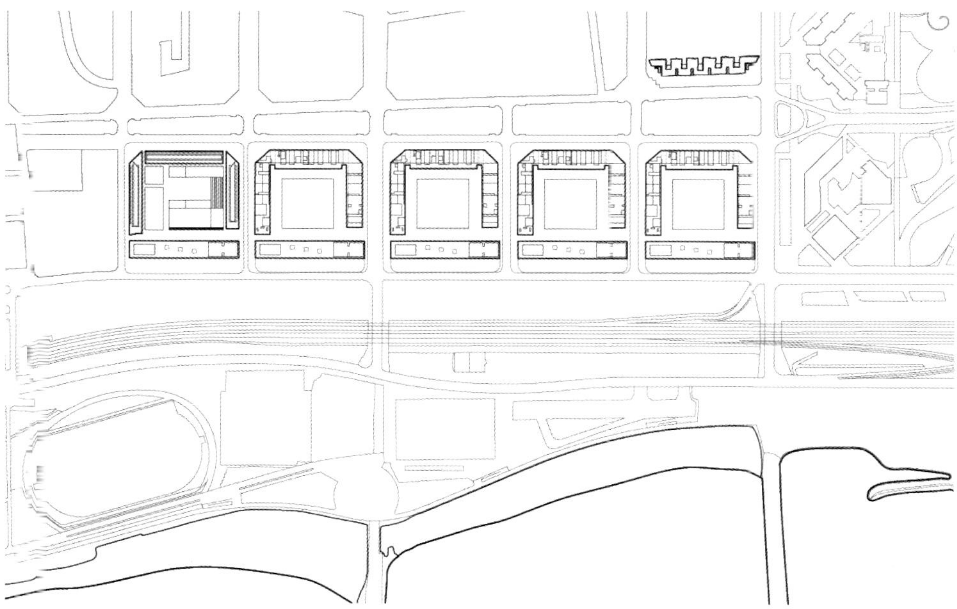

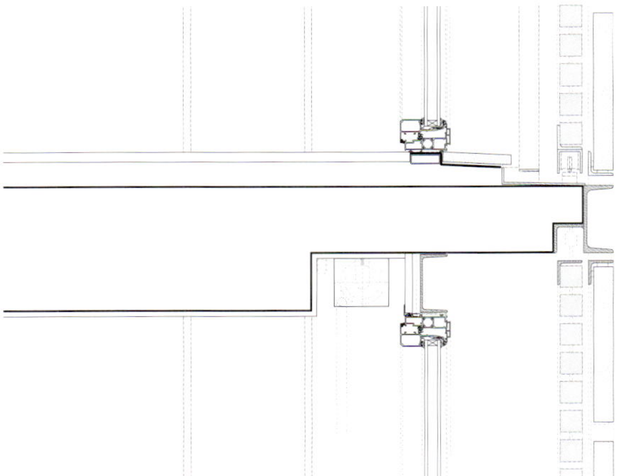

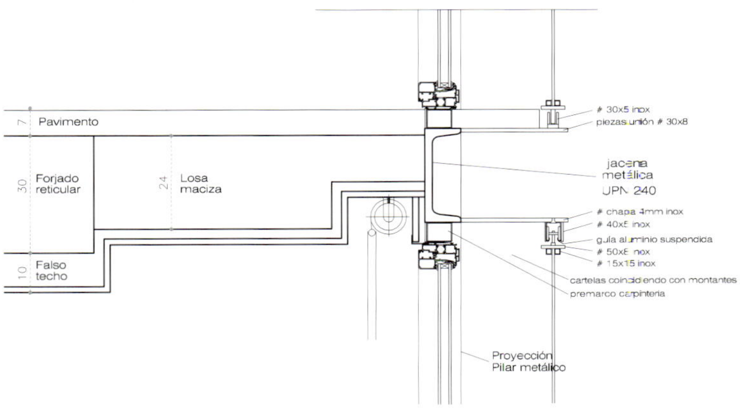

Balmes 145

València 381

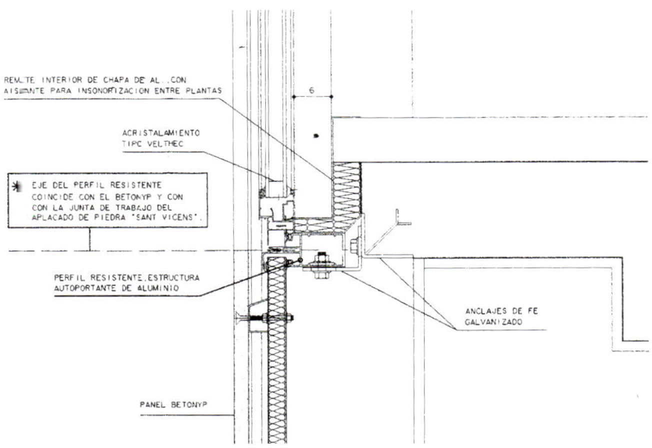

Gran Via 512

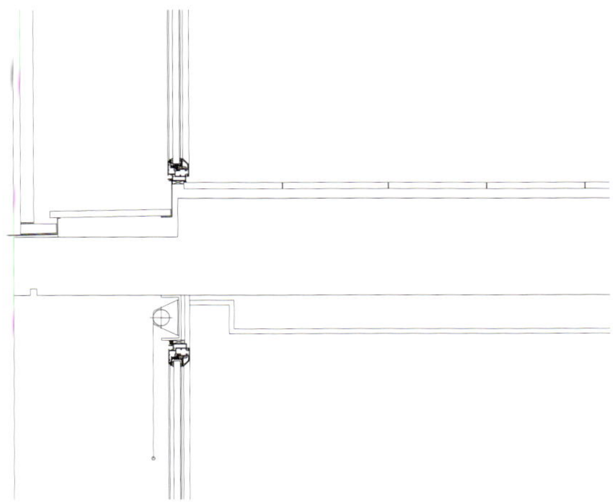

Roger de Flor 78

Housing building in Passeig de Gràcia 23 / Diputació 259

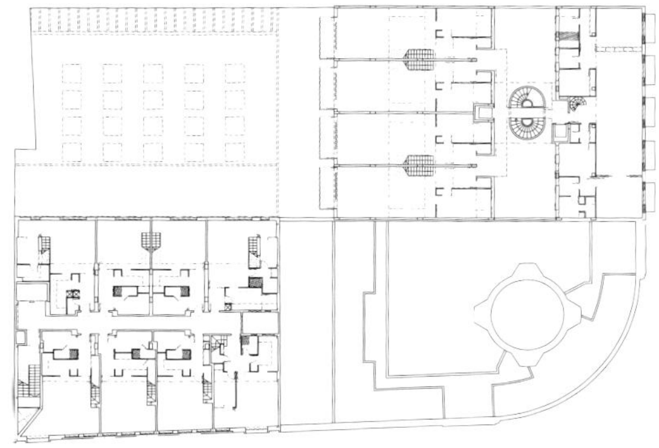

Typical floor plan

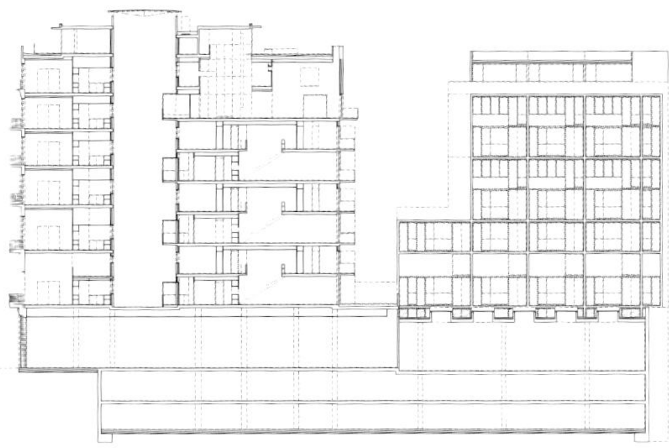

Section

Housing building in Passeig de Gràcia 99

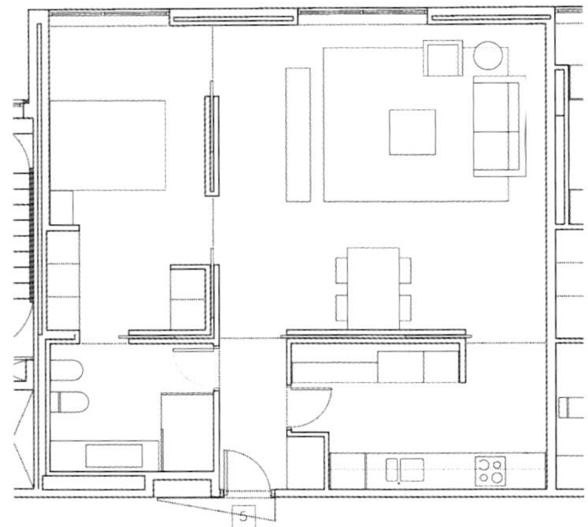

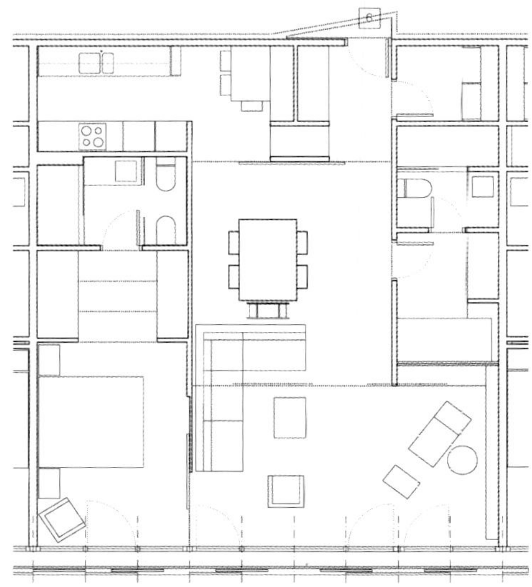

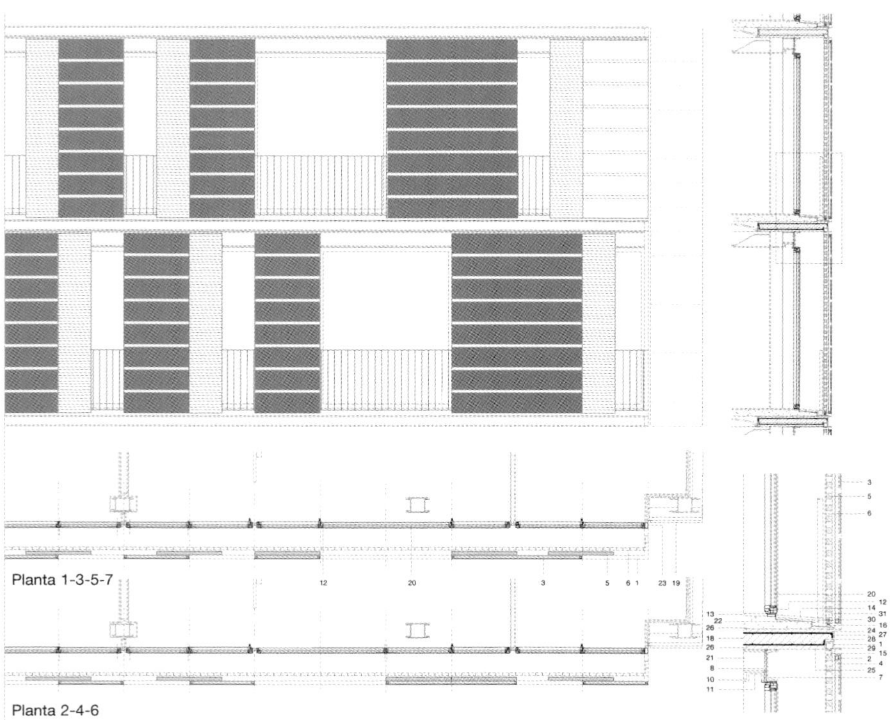

Planta 1-3-5-7

Planta 2-4-6

1. UPN 160 mm.
2. L 50x50x5 en acero inox. arenado.
3. Vidrio laminado 5+5 extraclaro con capa de mármol blanco portugal espesor total 15 mm.
4. Tubo 30x25 mm. en acero inox. chorreado.
5. Listones macizos de Sukupira.
6. Barandilla formada por pletinas de 40 mm. e= 6 mm. de acero para pintar.
7. UPN 240 mm. soldada a viga IPN 180 mm.
8. Aislante térmico de poliestireno extruido.
9. IPE 380 existente.
10. Falso techo pladur.
11. Cortinero de escayola.
12. Carpintería Technal Unicity color gris granulado.
13. Parquet flotante listones giordano.
14. Piedra natural.
15. Rodamiento de nylon.
16. Guía de acero inox.
17. UPN 160 mm.
18. Losa de hormigón de nueva construcción.
19. Piedra natural cogida con ganchos a la pared.
20. Vidrio laminado cámara laminado 4+4 silence + 10+5+5.
21. IPN 180 mm. soldada a pilares.
22. Impermeabilización.
23. L formada por pletinas de aluminic lacadas.
24. Goterón formado por chapa de acero doblada en acero inox. arenado.
25. Hormigón visto.
26. Armadura 1 Ø 8 c./15 superior e inferior soldada a vigueta existente.
27. Soldadura de la armadura superior al UPN.
28. Soldadura de la armadura inferior al angular L 60x6 mm.
29. Angular L 60x6 mm. soldado al UPN 160 mm.
30. Mortero de nivelación.
31. Rodamiento.

CIRCA
CIRCA
CIRCA

RABAT
99
RABAT

Hotel Mandarin Oriental in Passeig de Gràcia 38-40

MANGO
MANGO

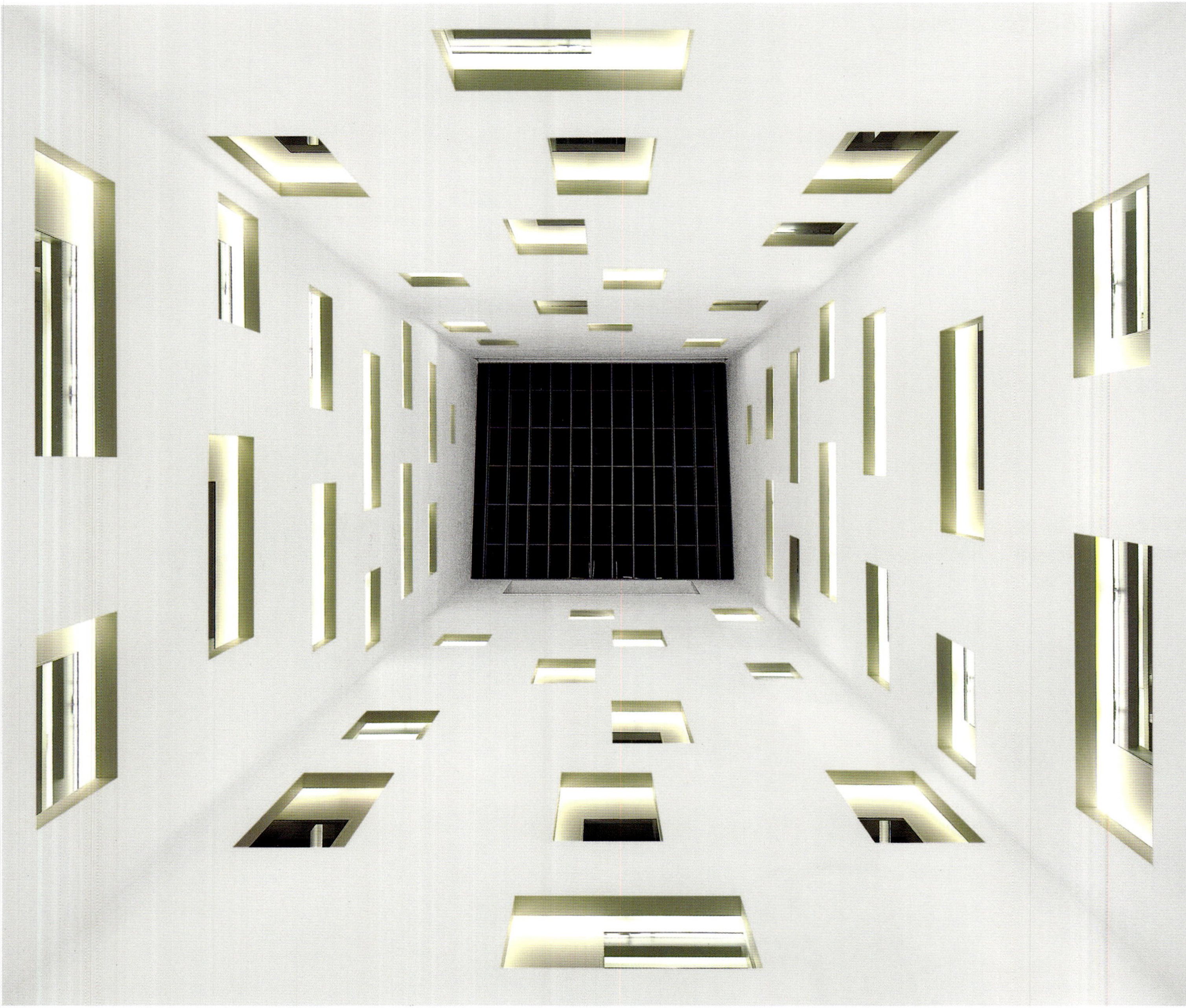

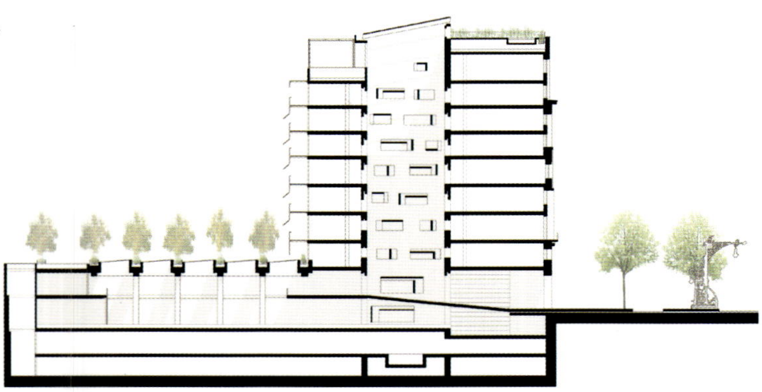

Longitudinal section

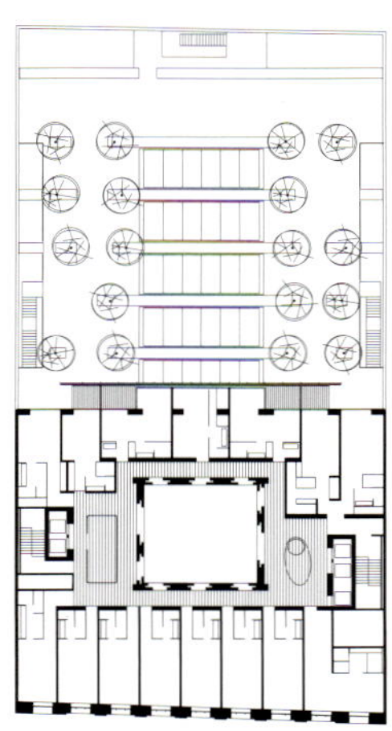

Typical floor plan

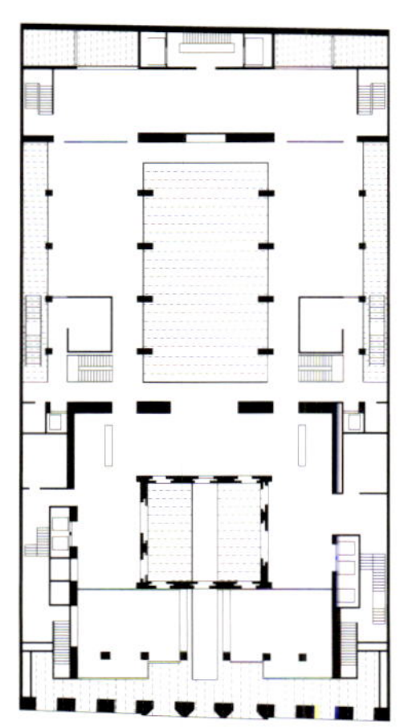

Mezzanine plan

Park and city

The first stages of the project design have been based on understanding the expansion of the Science Park as an opportunity to respond to issues of urban order that transcend the site and contribute to shaping an area of great importance to the city.

The relationship with the River Genil and the connection with adjacent spaces of centrality have been the mainspring of the project's urban dimension. From the start, the latter dismisses the idea of a totem building installed "above the city" and pays attention instead to the various locations of the edges and points of contact with what already exists.

These concerns have configured an organism that houses different types of space beneath a single roof, which, with slight inflections and an outer skin resembling that of a hand, enables the park and the city to occupy the intermediary spaces -between the fingers—which accommodate the components of the program. The footbridge linking the opposite bank of the Genil is the arm that brings the city into the park, a new pedestrian access that connects with points of intense activity, encounter and meeting.

A new way of traversing the Science Park *hors control* enables us to take in the complex from a high position and even to cross the lobby over the main skylight, while appreciating the space and the bustle on the inside, which, descending towards the access plaza, leads us to the entrance of the building and the ticket office area.

Interactivity

The idea of interactivity is present on all levels regarding the park. Spatial continuity and intensification of the interactive potential between building and city are the proposal's main theme. The enclosure shares its public dimension with the city by means of new urban routes that are interconnected with interior circulations.

Just as the Science Park focuses its attention on the interactive exhibition of its themed areas, so the project provides all visitors with spaces in which to move with total freedom, accessibility and continuity. Discovering the possible routes among the many options will convert the user into an interested and inquisitive individual who takes on an active role.

Flexibility

The proposed spatial structure allows for total flexibility of use and for diverse configurations interweaving routes and themed areas. This entails converting the experience of the space into an area for games and fun. Intersecting glances, a rapport with the landscape and confined spaces are revealed throughout the visit.

Spatial organization

The idea of an "enigmatic box" awakens curiosity and subtly displays its interior as an invitation to be discovered in prolongation with the space of the street.

A single undulating plane floats ten meters high and is sustained by the structure of the program's huge main boxes, defining in its interstices the vast space of the lobby, a permanent reference for both interior and exterior routes, underlined by the low-angled light of the façade windows and emphasized in the heart of the building by the great glazed fissure identifying the park on a metropolitan scale.

The main function of this lobby will be to lead and direct the visitor within the complex; it receives the flow of people from the access plaza and the green space next to the river and sends them to the extended open spaces already inside the enclosure: the Nature Plaza or Biodome, and the Observatory Plaza.

Suitable programmatic features intensify the porosity surrounding the complex: mini-cinemas, Internet cafés, a cyber library, and shopping areas are set out in continuity with the platform of the public green space constituted in the vestibule of the Cultural Gallery, from where people can also move onto the Macroscopio and the rest of the park. Accessibility is a basic premise of the entire circulation system.

Given its clear identity within the complex, the Al-Andalus Science Pavilion helps maximize the interactive aspect between the city and the Science Park. Its entrances are independent and include a public green space nearby. Light is the main rationale for organizing the spaces. Four skylights over four courtyards determine the interior, configuring a flexible base for the organization of the themed spaces.

Sustainability, recycling and collection

The new building becomes a genuine support of these contemporary statements, which are obligatory in large-scale public projects.

The choice of material fulfills technological innovation and energy-saving ecological criteria, supporting and simplifying maintenance and good conservation.

A new urban plane is configured—the large roof—as an abstraction of the furrowed textures of the Vega flatland. Sections of the roof are adapted to harness solar energy, permitting optimal heating and cooling costs. Other sections are containers for material recycled from building work and other industrial processes: ceramic, plastic, glass, concrete, and metal, which will be classified and processed in situ to become ballast and surfacing material.

01 Access
02 Auditorium
03 Cultural Gallery
04 Tecno-Forum Hall
05 Al-Andalus Pavilion and Science
06 Biodome
07 Temporary Exhibition Hall
08 Pavilion "Travel to the Human Body
09 Pavilion "Cultural Hall of Prevention"
10 Circulations
11 Garden Genil
12 Forest of Feelings

Hospital Inmaculada

URENDE
URENDE

Multi-housing in Bilbao

On Bilbao's Riverside

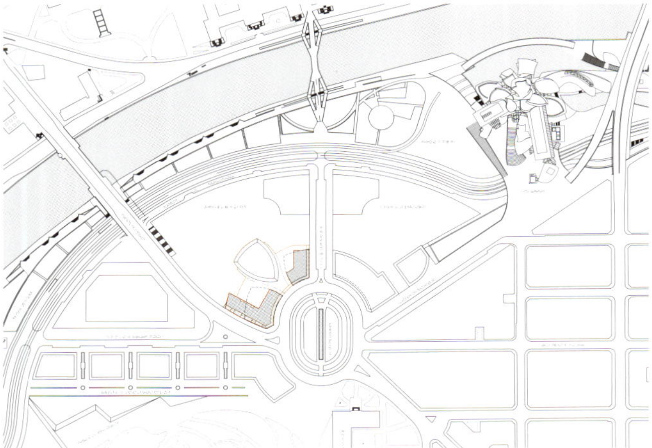

Block A. 7th Level

The IMQ Hospital in Bilbao

A building of a unitary, global kind that constructs a landscape, given that it has interiorized Bilbao's genetic code, determined by the modernity of a highly contemporary geometry and the industrial tradition of the city.

The project defines an envelope that binds together the different parts of this complex hospital program in the podium. Said program is defined by the abstract treatment of the outer skin, punctuated by structural ribs extending vertically up the entire height of the building. The flexible modulation allows for great versatility when it comes to subdividing the interior space.

The polygonal faade converts the hospitalization block into the icon of the building, responding to the location by becoming the gateway of the future remodeling of Zorrozaurre and configuring a new urban frontage on the estuary, in keeping with the Guggenheim and the Euskalduna Palace.

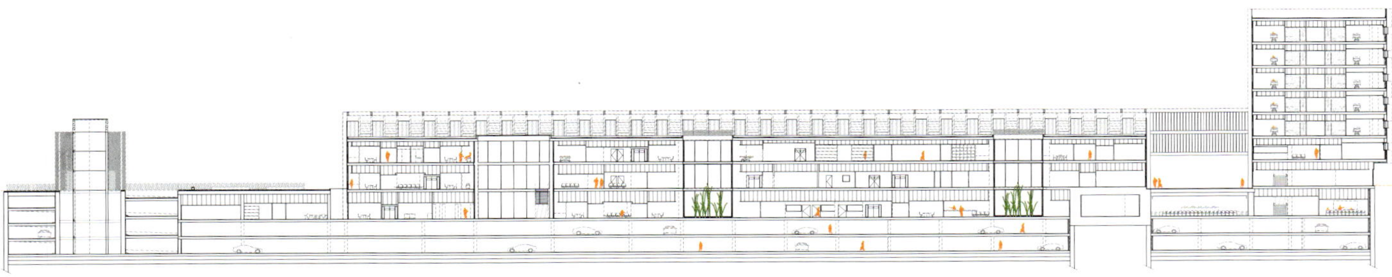

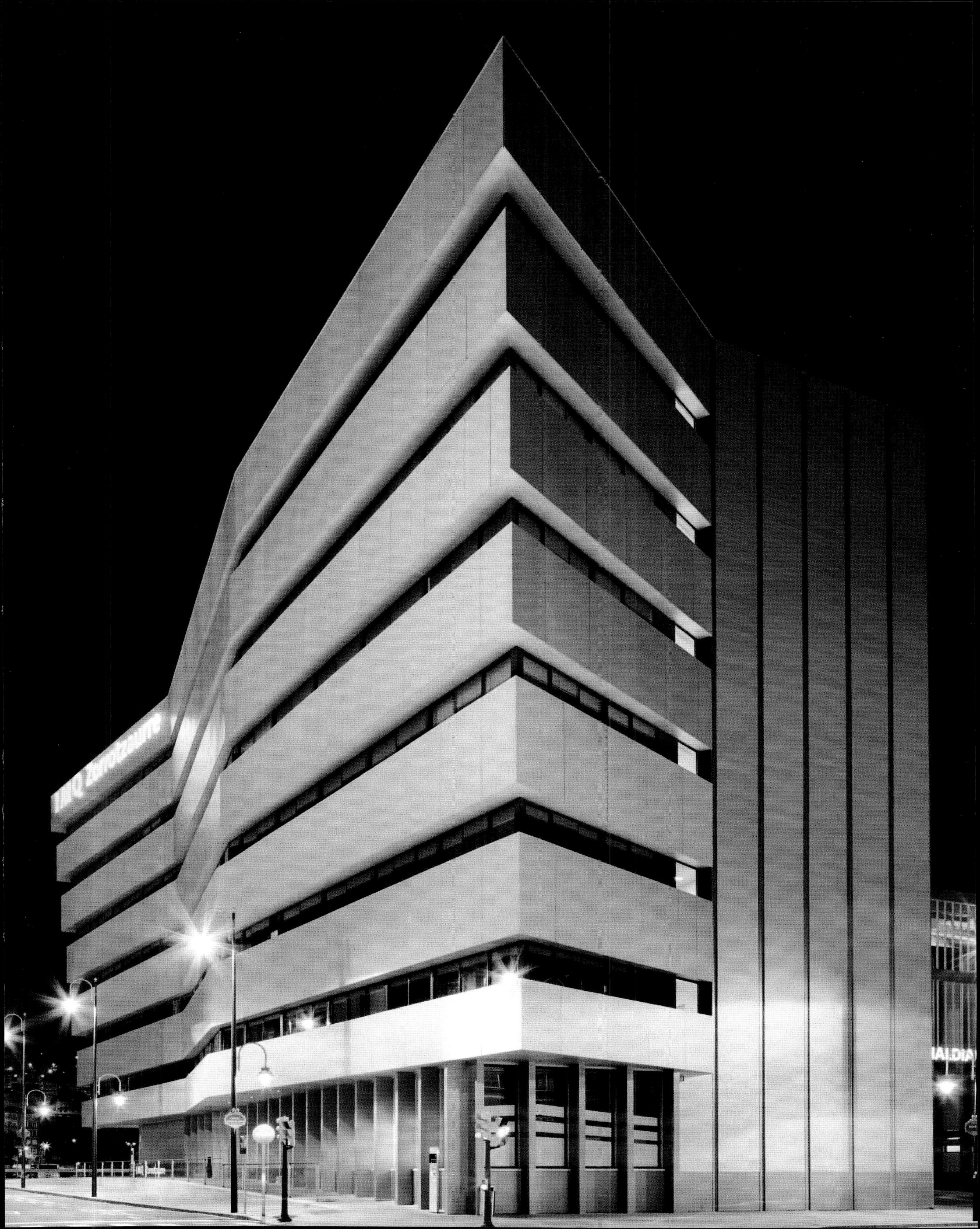

Between the sea and the Venetian Lagoon

Carlos Ferrater

The Italian experience

After graduating in the early 1970s from the Barcelona School of Architecture, virtually paralyzed by the political situation of the late-Franco regime, trips to northern Italy were a breath of fresh air because there, the world of architecture and design led by Gardela, Albini, Peresutti & Rogers, Ponti, Gregotti, and Magistretti, but also by designers like Sotsass, Colombo, Mendini and Zanusso, seemed to recognize or renew the legacy of the avant-garde rationalists of the 1930s, following on from the generation of Terragni, Moretti, Figini & Pollini, Ridolfi and Libera.

New Italian architecture genealogically reconstructed the line of succession, while in the School of Venice, Tafuri, Escolari, Aymonino, and Rossi formulated the theoretical bases of a new theory of the city, which in a few years would result in dogma blocking the future production of Italian architecture. By breaking the continuity of modern tradition that paradoxically re-emerged in Catalan architecture through the teachings brought to Catalonia by the creators of the School of Barcelona.

The exhibition at the Triennale di Milano of José Antonio Coderch de Sentmenat, and in particular the mediation of Oriol Bohigas, Federico Correa, and Ignasi de Solà-Morales, and a group of young teachers from the architecture school in Barcelona set the stage and planted the seed that in the 1980s and early 90s marked the emergence of Catalan architecture, and especially the urban transformation of Barcelona.

My memories of trips in the 1970s to northern Italy, preferably Milan and Venice, represent a time of learning, knowledge and familiarity of their cultural and historical models. In recent years Italy, and in particular the city of Venice, has been the most frequent destination of my visits, panels, project corrections, and conferences sponsored by Professor Eleonora Mantese in the Venice Institute of Architecture.

In the early years, still on the campus of San Polo, she showed us an off the beaten track Venice and thus a friendship formed that led us to collaborate in the competition for the extension of the *Cimitero de la isola de San Michele*.

We competed alongside David Chipperfield and Enric Miralles. I remember an extraordinary boat trip across the Venetian Lagoon along with Benedetta Tagliabue in which we were shown the old cemetery, its secrets, and problems such as the slow mineralization its incumbents due to the humidity and pollution of the sludge drained from the Venetian canals and used in its construction. Years later, in the new Cottonifficcio School, we did a design workshop in the summer of 2004 with Eleonora Mantese, Christiana Eusepi,

Design competition for the Isola de San Michele cemetery

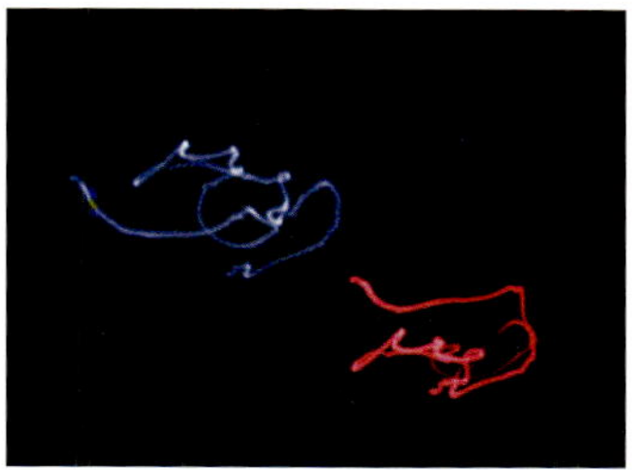

Kites flying in the night skies over Venice

Workshop in Venice with Eleonora Mantese

and Gustavo Carabajal, and I remember the exciting night flight of the "aquilones" constructed by students on the canals of Venice. After the academic collaboration, I asked Eleonora and Gustavo to collaborate on the project, sponsored by the Veneto planning consultant, Danilo Gerotto, a private Venetian developer who had the idea to carry out the project from a public/private agreement on the Lido di Jesolo, which consisted of the renovation of public space in the center of the town and the construction of facilities and services that would frame the Aquileia Tower—a 100 meters tall, it would be by far the highest tower in the Venetian landscape.

Located between the mouth of the River Sile and Piave, between the sea and the lagoon, the project built in part through the efforts and dedication of Gustavo Carabajal, its profile has become the new emblem of the town.

In recent years, after being awarded a Doctor Honoris Causa from the University of Trieste in February 2006, our new studio has been invited to participate in several competitions in various locations in Italy. As a result, we are currently working with Domenico Piemonte on projects such as the remodeling of Castello Borelli and its hydraulic devices, in which we proposed the creation of a small residential settlement in the form of a plaza suspended over the sea in a fissure in Monte Piccaro between the towns of Borghetto and Cerialli in the region of Liguria. This project, together with our recent work, has been exhibited at the invitation of Ordine degli Architetti di Roma in the magnificent Roman Aquarium in Rione Monti, throughout September, an exhibition curated by Paolo Maselli, one of our studio's partners.

Project for the remodelling of Castello Borelli, Liguria

During the 2009-2010 academic year, together with Alberto Peñín, and with the collaboration of Stella Rahola and Jordi Vidal, we have developed proposals for the new port in Venice next to the church of Santa Elena, in the context of the Projects XXI Master's Degree which we teach for the Fundació UPC in the OAB gallery and in the School of Architecture of Barcelona.

For us Italy has been, and will be in the coming years, our favorite destination in terms of our work, both for its cultural proximity and affinity with many young architects who have been carrying out their apprenticeship in our studio, and for their renewed interest in the contemporary project.

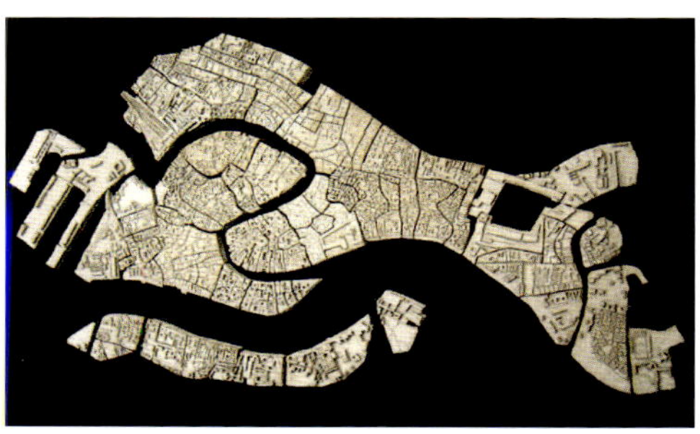

"Projects XXI" Master's Degree. Scale Model of Venice in clay

The project falls between the Venice Lagoon, the mouth of the Rivers Sile and Piave, and the sea, and is integrated through an axis perpendicular to the coastline. It extends from the Piazza Internazionale, Via Aleardi, Piazza Mazzini, Via Bafile and the beach, sticking four hundred meters out into the sea. The system of penetration is an alternative to the traditional longitudinal system typical of this area.

An underground public parking lot in Piazza Internazionale with a tree-lined path that alternates between sun and shade, the remodeling of Via Aleardi with the formation of a new public space, the 2,000 m^2 Piazza Aquileia, surrounded by a twin-level building that contains various commercial uses and facilities such as shops, cafes, restaurants and fitness and a sun terrace and pool. A passage serves as the entrance to the underground parking and the logistics of the tower and shopping complex. In the middle of this space surrounded by these buildings stands the Aquileia Tower, one hundred meters tall.

The project includes the regeneration of the Piazza Mazzini, at the junction of Via Aleardi and Bafile, as a space that organizes the intervention. The plaza is thought of as a changing space which supports various uses. This place, paved in stone with trees and lighting, a large bench, and a set of sprinklers, sprays and fountains, allows for a multitude of uses and control of the road traffic, as well as multiple environmental possibilities. On the south side of the plaza, a large window onto the sea, shaped by residential buildings and a quay in the form of a promenade that sticks out into the sea and creates a small dock for the occasional mooring of small boats, completes the intervention.

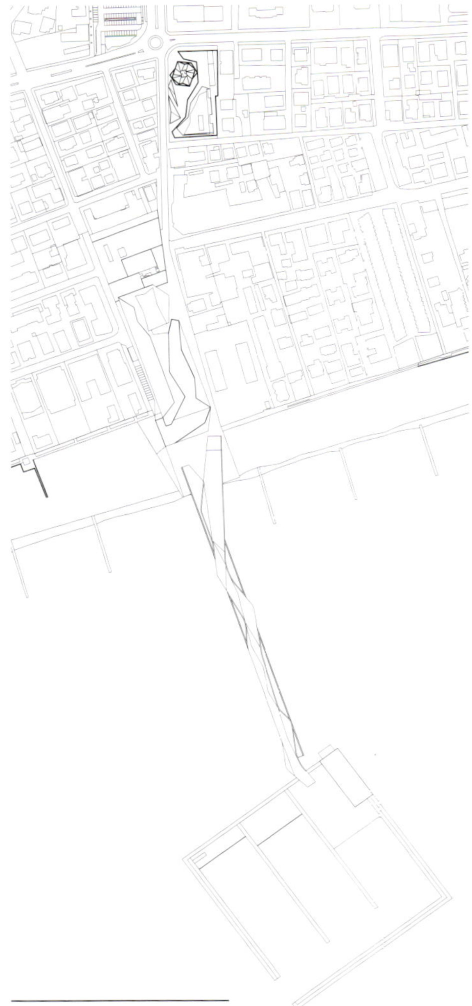

Intervention plan

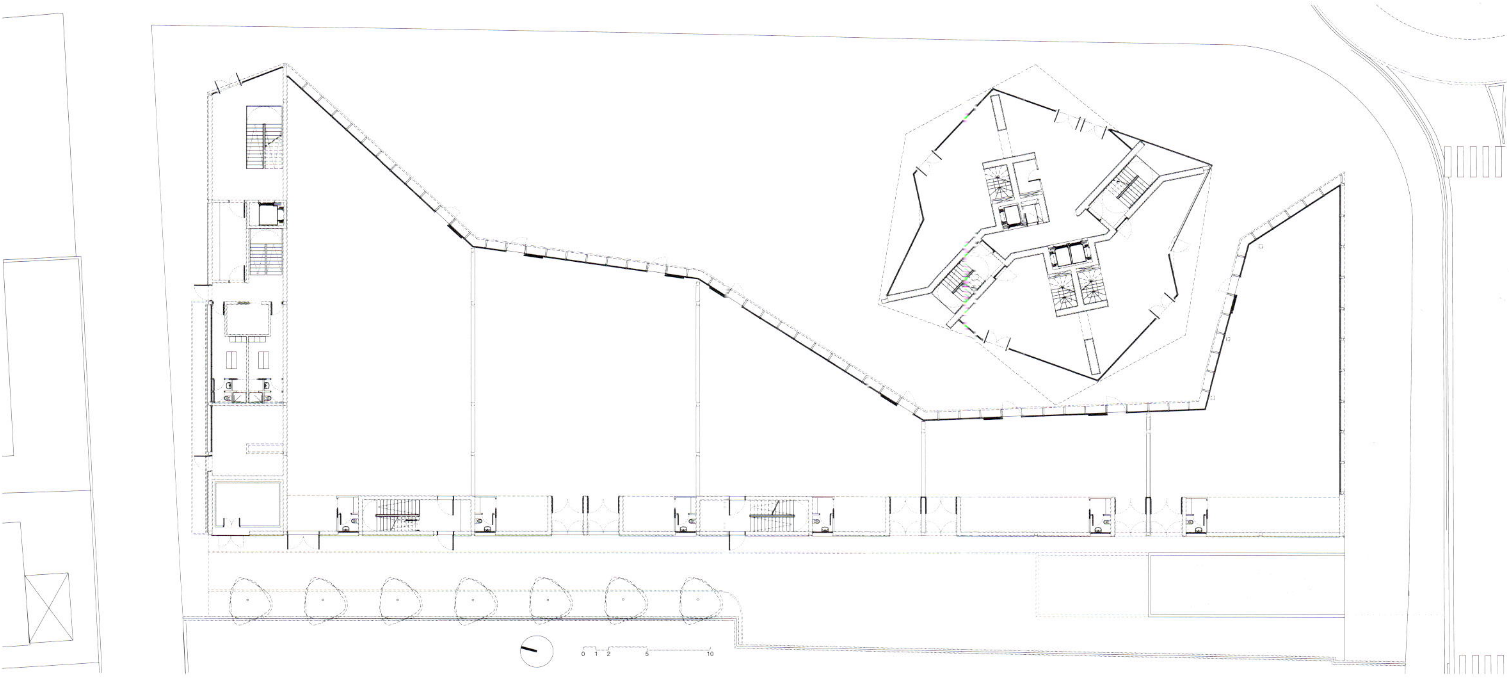

Piazza Aquileia plan

The 24-story Aquileia Tower is structured with a double-height ground floor housing the lobby, banks and a cafeteria, two floors for offices and twenty-two floors with different residential apartments. The polygonal profile organized around the vertical circulation cores, lifts and emergency staircases, provides the four apartments on each floor, of which two are one-bedroom and two are two-bedroom, with views from the terraces of both the sea and lagoon. The houses facing west have views of the campaniles (bell towers) and the city center of the city of Venice, while the apartments facing east offer views of the rivers and the distant horizon of the Dolomites.

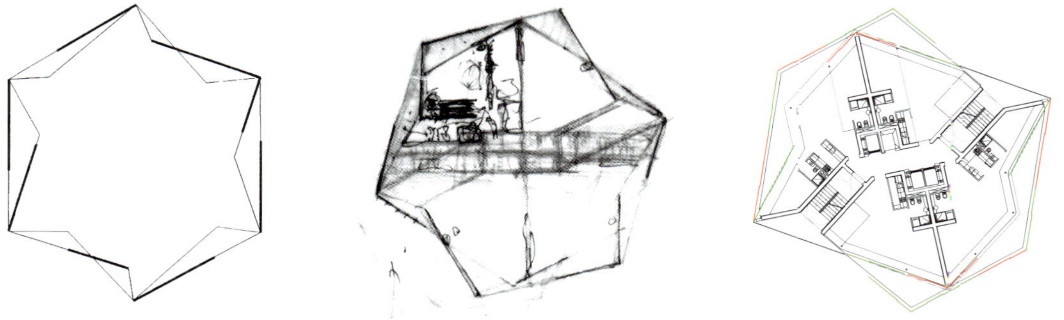

This configuration means that privacy is maintained while allowing for the construction of the Intermediate, i.e. interior-exterior, spaces. These polygonal-shaped terraces become living spaces. An extension of the home, their use is made more flexible through sliding glass walls and blinds, becoming a real environmental and climate filter, adjusting the light and shade, and the views. The ensemble of the façades is a lightweight, subtle and versatile material that causes the skin to dematerialize, while maintaining the tectonic image of the tower.

The building is crowned with two outstretched sail-shaped pinnacles, which when lit up at night become a nighttime landmark from afar. They act as structural brackets attached to the concrete nucleus, supported through tensors that force the projections of the façade perimeter to work by traction.

On the ground floor, large glass expanses hide the structure and help balance the volume of the tower with the stony surface of the plaza. The apartments of 60 and 75 m^2, with terraces between 20 and 30 m^2, consist of an access program, living room, dining room, kitchen, and one or two bedrooms with their respective bathrooms.

In summary, the Aquileia Tower project, as a Veneto-wide iconic entity , offers a recognizable profile in an area of low-rise building, playing with the fog and the light of the Adriatic area, and becomes the main argument of a new urban system focusing on centrality.

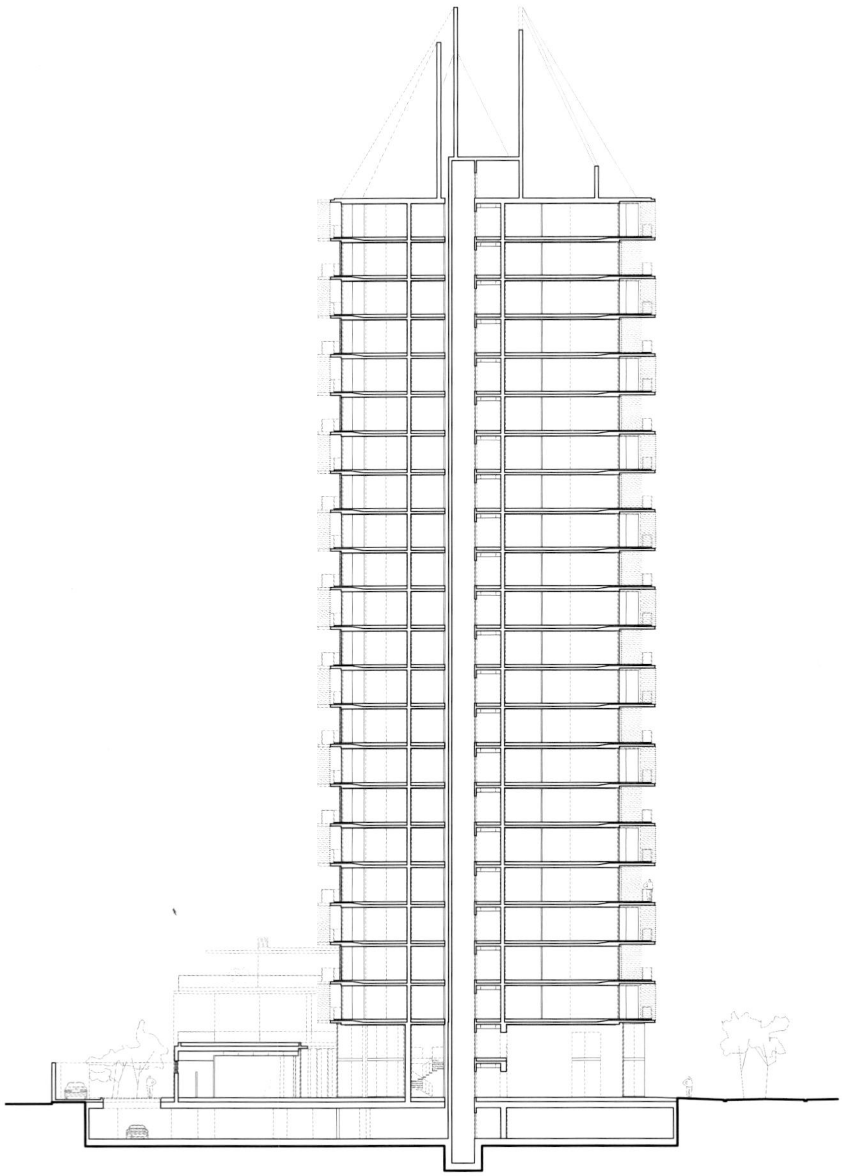

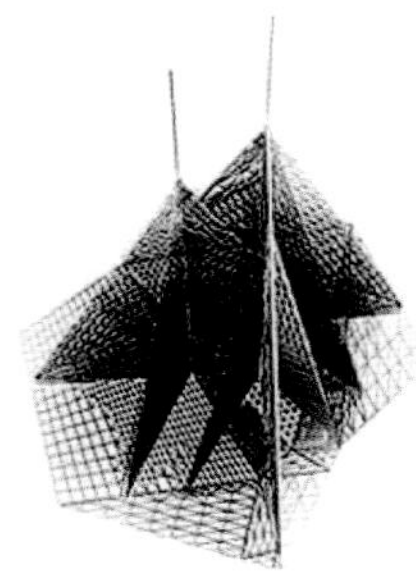

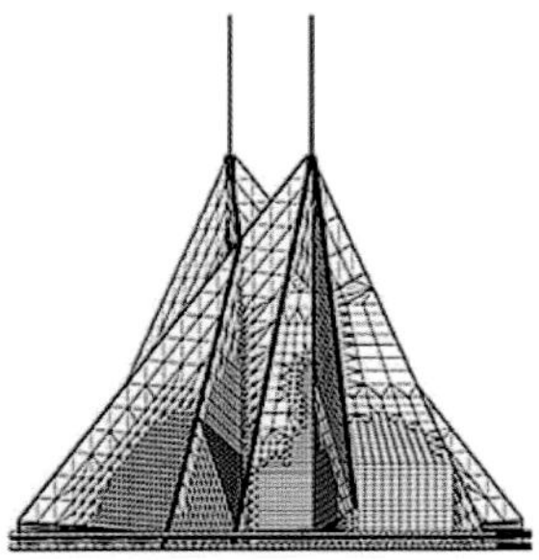

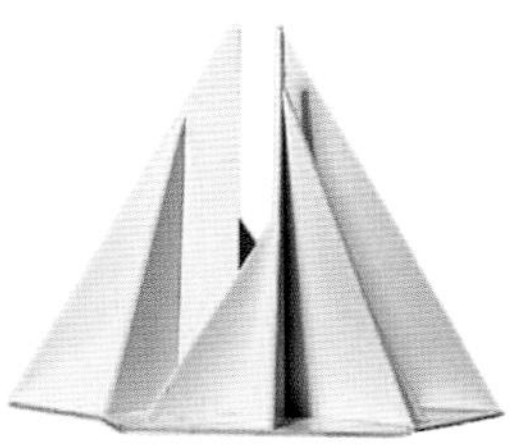

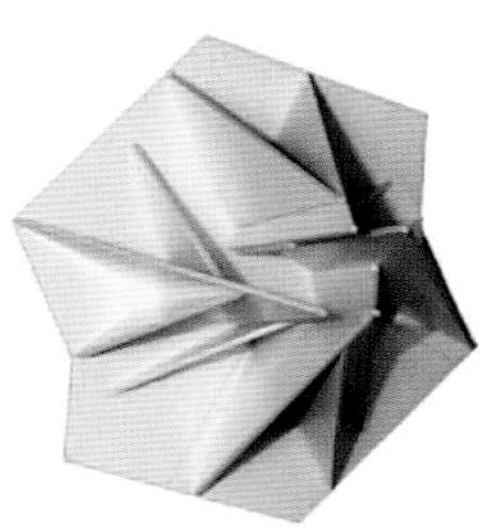

Section

Non profit

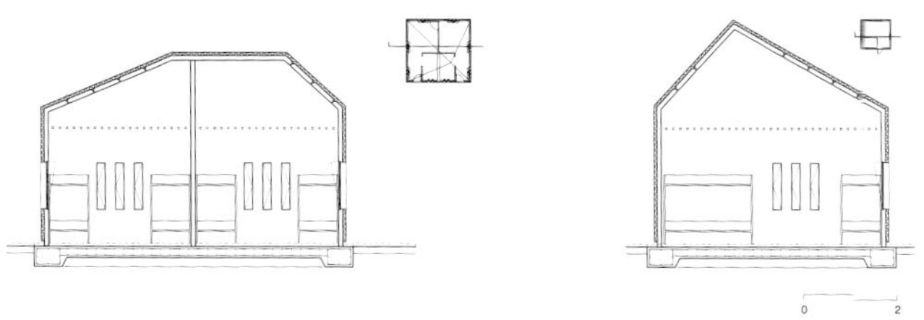

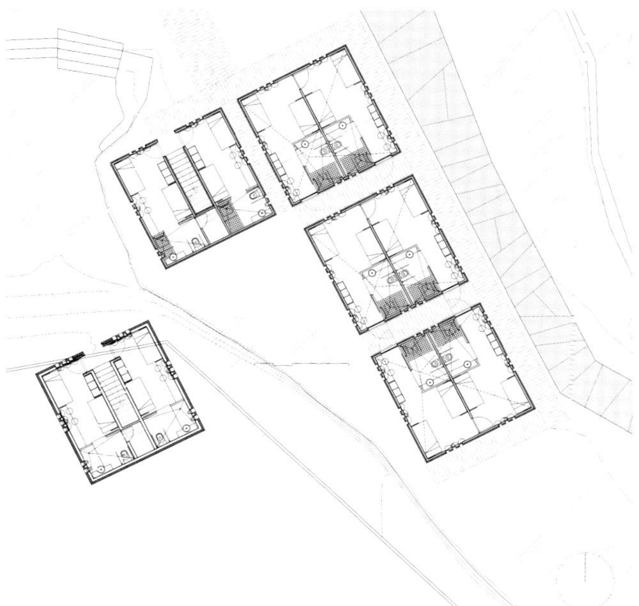

NGO Centre Esplai

Breaking away from the conventional types of holiday home which keep to the "side-by-side" schema, we propose to create individual units that will all relate to each other yet still remain autonomous units.

The ratio of floor area increases, and communication between the units is possible through outside walkways. Volumetric fragmentation allows small autonomous units to graduate the number of users and minimize the costs of maintenance and supervision, while allowing configuration of a system within the whole colony.

The unit is proposed as a benchmark archetype and image of the imaginary world of childhood: small houses, small people, rapport with the forest, roads, and nature that allow for easy extension and expansion of the system itself. Exterior routes adapt to the paths between the different volumes and allow circulation between them by grouping entrances and facilitating control by the monitors.

We propose three different room types, with groups of four, six or eight children, with the opportunity to develop a level or two as the body, resulting in the end of a total capacity of ninety places. The upper space and volume of air has assumed great importance, given that the ambience of the rooms favors the incorporation of acoustic control and artificial illumination provided by white tube lighting suspended from the ceiling.

The simplicity of the materials used has permitted greater economic viability by means of implementation, final impact, and subsequent maintenance. In the interiors, bare, painted, and polished concrete block floors of fine particle size, window widths of 20 cm embedded in matt stainless steel frames 2mm thick with painted shutters, incorporated to darken the interior, and tongue-and-groove jointed domes all come together to give a warm tone to the interior light.

The location of the sets of vertical windows provides perfect cross-ventilation, regardless of the prevailing wind in each case. For the exterior, the uniqueness in the materials of the façades and roofs, in both the cellular rooms and public buildings, a flexible and self-cleaning stucco that permits continuity and insulation around the water-repellent treated perimeter.

The final proposed solution allows for a broad spectrum of users; not just schoolchildren summer campers, but also families and groups who will want NGO Centre Esplai to use the camp facilities all year round.

Azahar: A Sustainable Building

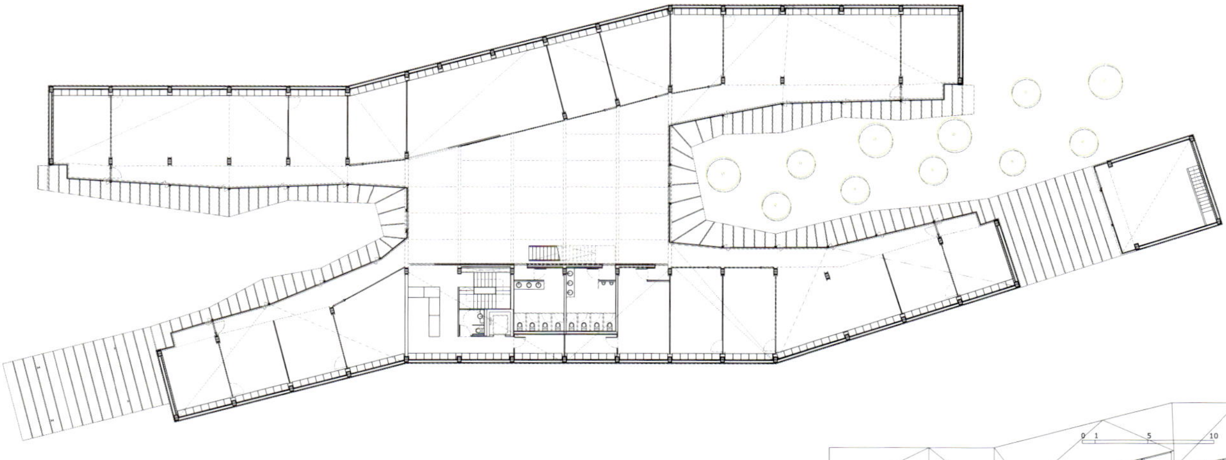

Ground floor plan

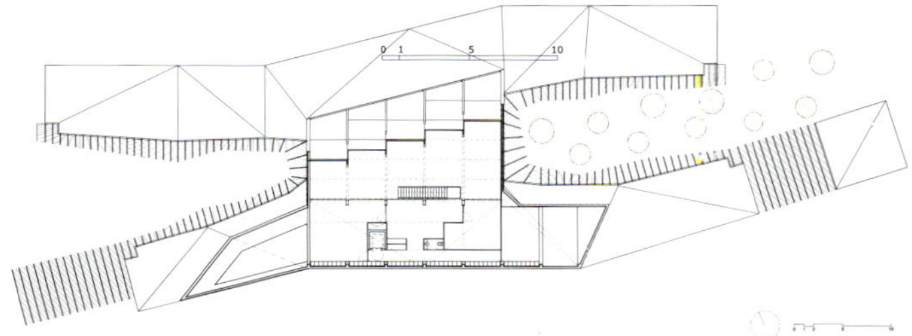

Mezzanine plan

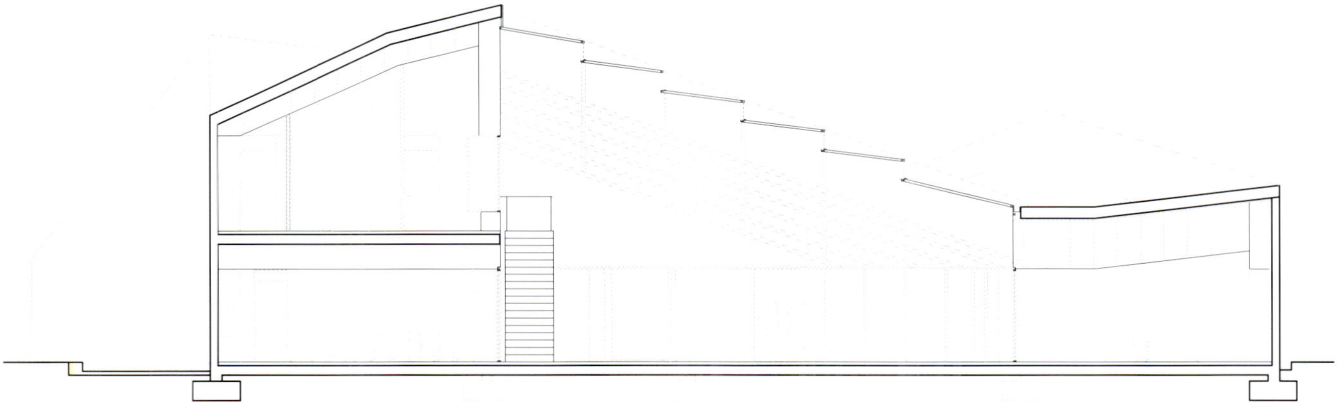

Cross sections

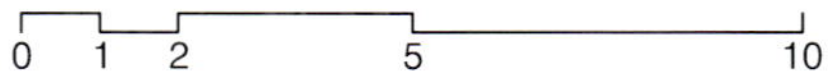

Urban actions

Alenti Hotel

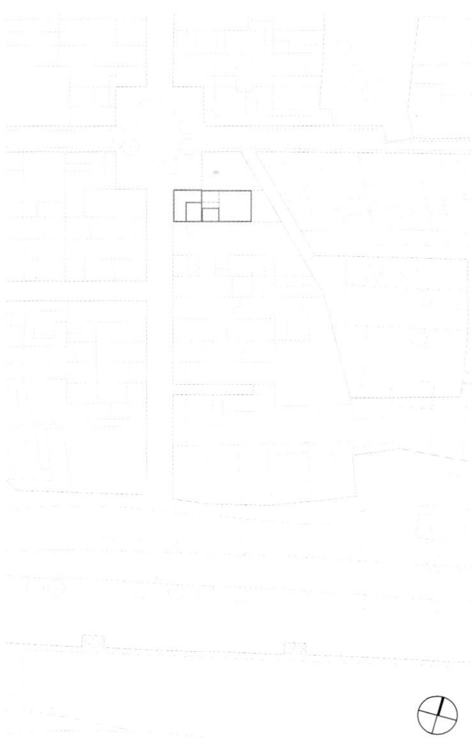

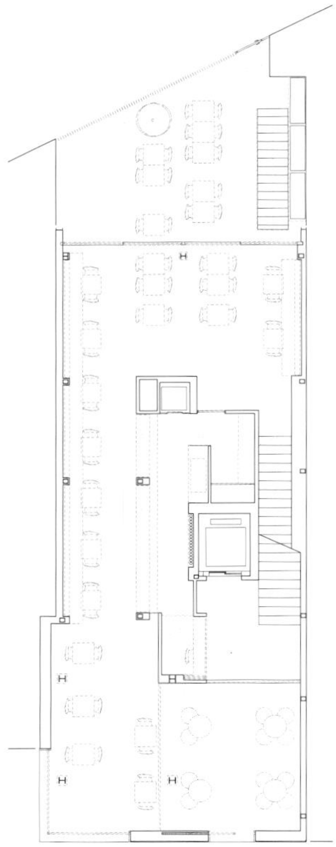

Ground floor plan

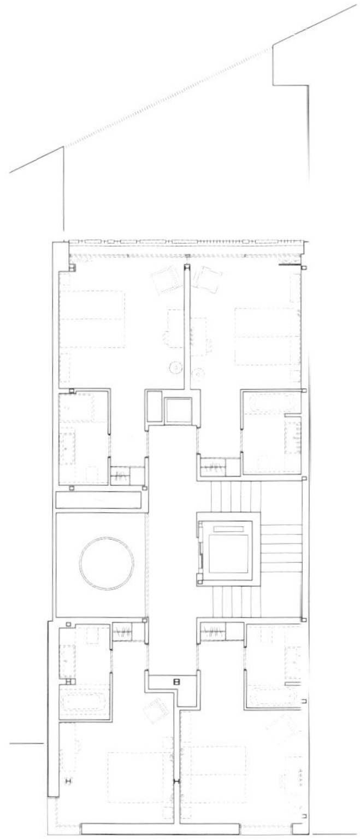

Typical floor plan

restaurante
hotel
ALENTI
CERVEZA

Hotel Alenti, Sitges

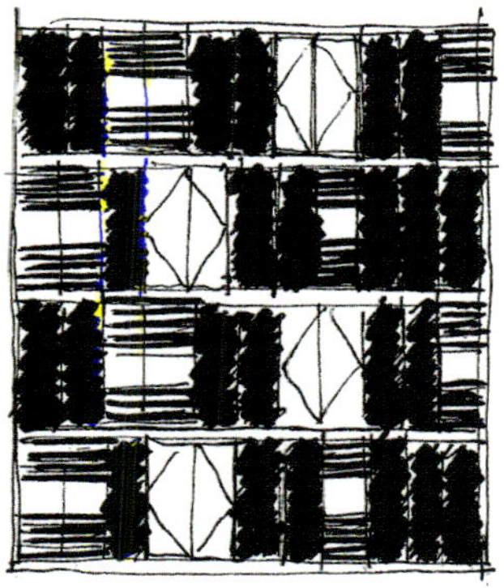

Two projects offered us a strict program defined by the end-users, and, in particular, the desire to have a representative and singular building in their urban setting.

The first, a nine-room hotel, is located on the corner of a central square in Sitges, which responds to a layout of narrow and irregular streets lined with low buildings. The location is the famous Carrer 2 de Maig or "Sin Street," so-called because of its nightlife. The client was a developer and friend, and his young and enterprising daughter who had recently returned from the US and who, after a number of years spent on cruise ships, decided to settle down and take over the family business. The need arose to construct a contemporary building that took into account the Mediterranean tradition and the concepts of the local vernacular architecture. The building is an attempt to dignify a public space by enhancing the value of the corner, using a sculptural composition of gaps and voids, reflective surfaces and transparency.

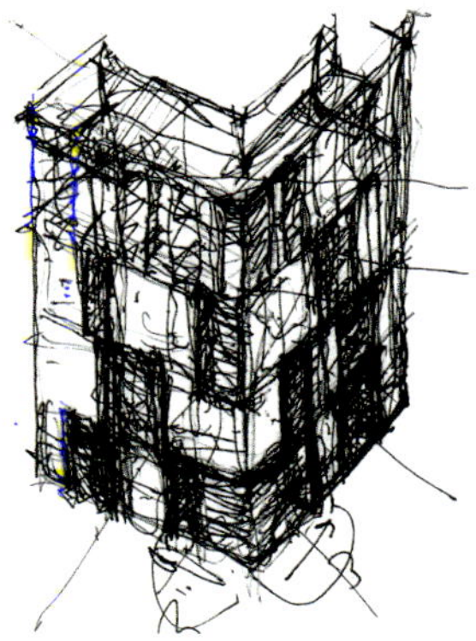

The second is a Protestant church for the United Evangelical Church of Terrassa, an institution with almost one hundred years of history in the town. This community, one of the largest of its kind in Catalonia, had been struggling to find a site for a building that would combine religious and social uses. It needed to house an auditorium and a library for the Protestant Archive of Catalonia, in addition to classrooms, music rooms, a multi-purpose space, and a childcare center to serve the district. The project took several months to design, during which close contact was maintained with the community, at times with long and well-attended meetings in the office, and at others in exhibiting the project in churches with 300 people. The new complex was paid for with the sale of the old building, with contributions from members of the community, and with a part granted by the government in return for commitment to the social project they would carry out.

The desire to have an austere but friendly building, without becoming an icon, yet at the same time unique and a reference point from a distance, led us to design a single-story entity without architectural barriers.

Due to the slope of the side streets, the height of the building was reduced and two cube-shaped volumes suspended over it, volumes which became representative on account of their size and their skin design. This new complex is located in an area between peripheral residential areas and the industrial area, where the plots are larger and the streets wider. It was opened by the former US President and Nobel Peace Prize-winner Jimmy Carter.

This church is the last in this overview of different situations we have found in urban centers, where small actions ranging from projects in low-density residential areas to public spaces with diverse programs have offered us the opportunity to experiment with design approaches involving the economizing of means, environmental efficiency, social organization, and respect for the built-up environment and for the city.

Evangelical Church of Terrassa

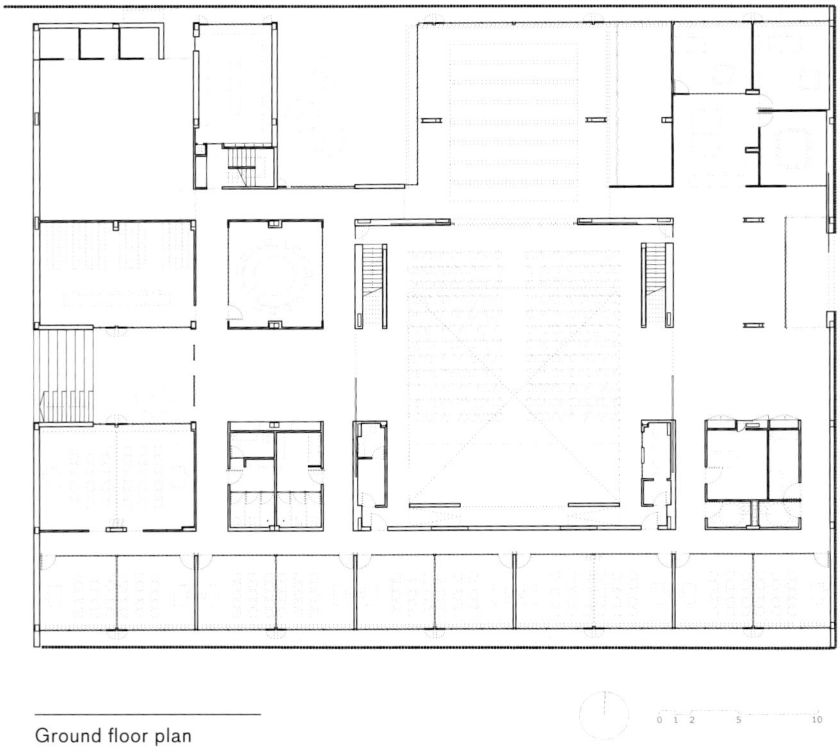

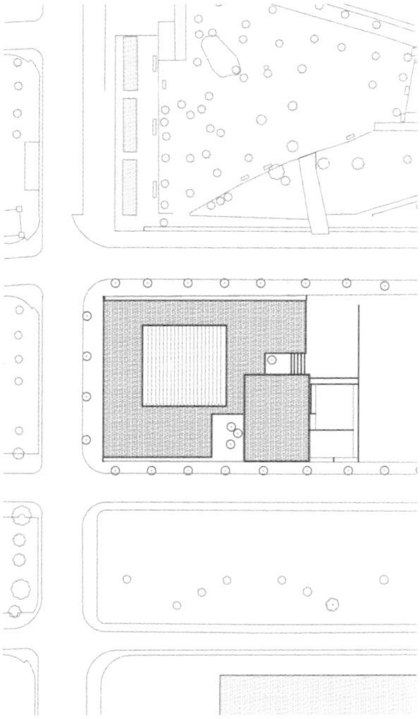

Ground floor plan

The United Evangelical Church of Terrassa, Barcelona, is located in the part of Can Tusell that faces Avainguda Bejar. The building combines religious and social uses, following an agreement with the city.

The complex is expressed as a large base with two volumes suspended above it, formed of steel plates that cover the façade on one side and become a fence on the other two sides, with decreasing height due to the slope of the land lot. In the central part of the building there appears a large cube with well-defined edges, which houses the sanctuary, being made of recycled aluminum scraps that lend a symbolic character to the geometric shape through their light-reflecting properties. The other, shorter cube beside Carrer Tramuntana is suspended and cantilevered. In this case, the defined edges mark the planes of perforated, corrugated aluminum lattice that act as a second skin for the child-care program.

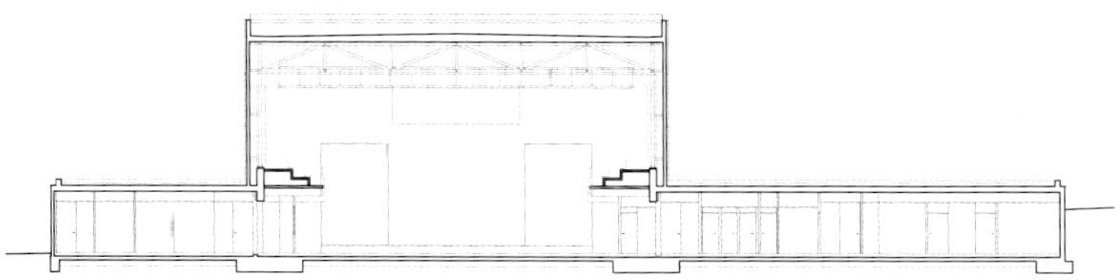

Cross section

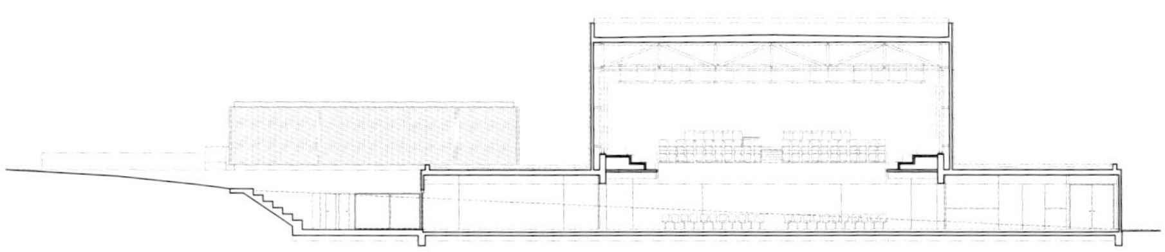

Longitudinal section

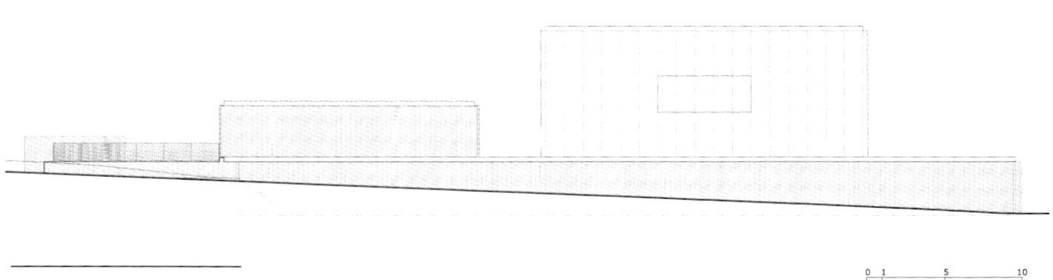

West elevation

The Michelin Headquarters in Boulogne-Billancourt. Paris

Longitudinal section

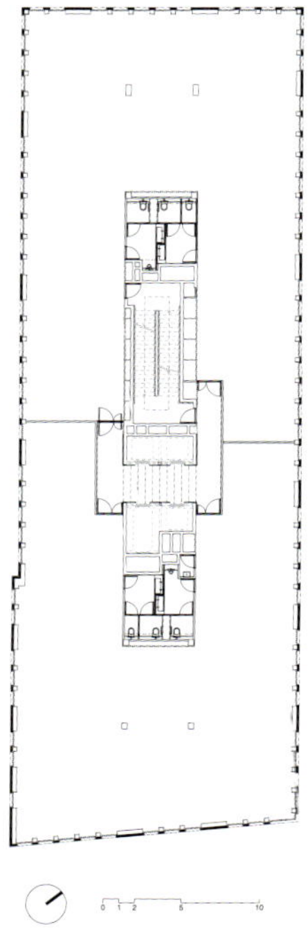

Typical floor plan

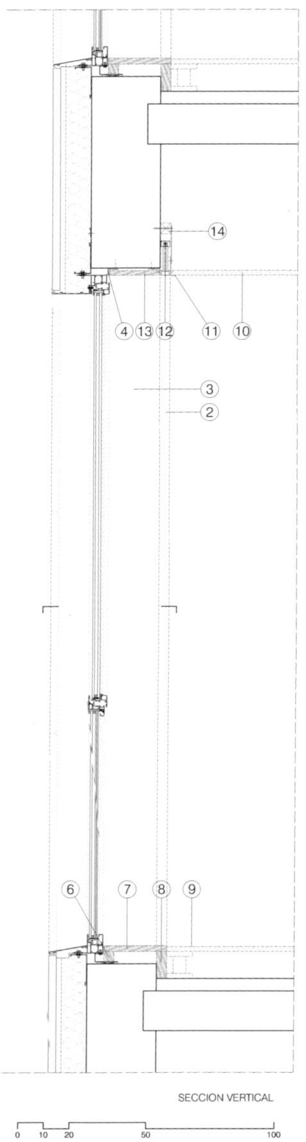

Wall. Vertical section

1 Bottom Panel lacquered wood. Hidden fixations. 245x24mm
2 Top lacquered wood boards. Fixed on board. 40x28mm
3 Panel lacquered wood. Hidden fixations, 205x16mm
4 Fixing galvanized steel.
5 Base board of lacquered wood. 20x24mm on wooden stick 110x40mm
6 Wooden stick 40x50mm
7 Support on lacquered wood. Hidden fixations. 205x16mm
8 Wooden stick 110x40mm
9 False ground on plots
10 Removable false ceiling
11 Continuous steel side profile, lacquered in white. 20x75mm
12 Stor with adjustable horizontal slats. Metallic silver. Crank
13 Top panel lacquered wood. 205x19mm. Hidden fixations. 205x19mm
14 Fixation of continuous steel side profile over the false ceiling.

The attention to the city postulated here is once again the initial argument behind the Boulogne-Billancourt building. Located on a bend in the Seine facing the Meudon Hills and with the Île Séguin as a river port, the former Renault factory site has been designated a regeneration area (*Zone d'aménagement concerté*), managed by SAEM Boulogne-Billancourt. This gradual redevelopment process will result in a new district that combines density, multiple uses, a restricted variety of building types, and the constant presence of the river landscape. It brings different owners and developers together in an operation overseen by the public authorities by means of design competitions for every large-scale development block. Architects such as Perrault, along with other offices, Nouvel, Foster, Diener&Diener, FOA, Mateo, Barani, and Baumschlager-Eberle are involved in the design. The first project designed and built by OAB in France, coordinated by the Belgian architect Stéphane Beel, was the outcome of one of these competitions.

Located in the avenue leading to Île Séguin, the project reformulates the construction density of the master plan to improve its relationship with the river to the south and to the north with the city of Paris, and with the commercial thoroughfare that will connect to the existing densely populated residential area. Faced with the diversity of the plan in terms of urban development and construction, the project proposes a classic and restrained modernity, in keeping with the town hall of Boulogne-Billancourt, one of the last projects by Garnier (1934), or even with the Institute Français building (1975) by Coderch in Barcelona, in a sort of return trip. The abstraction and timelessness exuded by the building contributes to its integration in the urban setting and is the architects' strategy for working in a responsible and dedicated manner abroad.

The choice of a silvery phyllite stone module measuring 45 x 90 x 3 cm came from the effectiveness on the floor plan of having a row of 1.35 m offices. These modules were submultiples of the 90 x 270 cm window, deeply inset with a 1 cm-wide extruded aluminum perimeter frame. The communications core, services, plant, and structural frame are laid out along a longitudinal axis, freeing a surface area of 18 x 54.5 m. The façade was built in France in concrete and houses and optimizes the rest of the structure. The stone and window modules clad this perimeter over a variable pentagram base, with slight variations and seemingly random gaps which, in some cases such as the cantilever, obey a structural logic.

Subtle changes appear at the top (ninth floor), where the modules are of a greater height and there are brise-soleils; on the corner of Avenue Île Séguin, where the windows are set at an angle; and on the ground floor, where the vertical proportion of the void is emphasized and the commercial premises are set back for greater protection and depth. The 5.50 m cantilever next to the residential building by Stéphane Beel provides continuity to the landscaped axis that crosses all the blocks, thus enhancing the lively commercial activity desired by the local authorities.

Four canopies are integrated into the building's exterior design to mark the entrance between stainless-steel frames. They consist of a horizontal plane suspended by cables, compressing space like an antechamber to the dual-aspect foyer that opens onto the landscaped slope at the heart of the block. The interior design is completed with silvery stone facing on the lifts, matt stainless steel on their frames and joinery, American oak paneling and front desk, and integrated indirect lighting.

The façade becomes an urban texture continuing onto the street, and establishes numerous associations with the Parisian sky and rain, with its material being alive and ambivalent, dark or silvery in line with the weather and light in the city. The quality of the stone, the random lights from offices at night, and reflections off the steel canopies and anodized aluminum frames contribute to dematerialize this petrous architecture.

MICHELIN
27

30
CÉDEZ LE PASSAGE

Corporate Buildings

The Audiovisual Campus in 22@ District. Mediapro

Carlos Ferrater

Building with steel

The evolution of architecture over time can be understood as a series of innovations in the way of building, and of new materials which have enabled architects from different periods to yoke their ideological positions, intellectual challenges, and technological advances to the search for new forms of expression.

Exposed steel skeletons became structural diagrams in which it was possible to understand the relation of stress, bending, compression and traction, creating new aesthetics in which engineering and architecture turned cast-iron and steel into a paradigm of modernity. Hidden skeletons, like that of Adler and Sullivan's Auditorium Building in Chicago, gave rise to standardized construction methods and the creation of density in urban centers, defining a new city model and consecrating verticality as a new formal experience.

Mies van der Rohe rediscovered steel; he rigidified joints and gave rigor, order, proportion, and meaning to the metal structural frame. His works in Chicago, New York, and Berlin have a steel frame uniting and bringing timelessness to the classicism/modernity duality, creating in the hidden part of the design process the conditions for the resulting materiality of his buildings.

Given its malleability and versatility, its ability to support all sorts of stress, and the ease with which it is used in building, steel has also allowed a range of works to be erected that mask absurd structures and arbitrary forms behind stone renderings and light metal and glass skins, thereby producing self-absorbed objects that do not respond to urban situations. They do not build a city. Their functional programs do not respond to proper social organization, and they exceed the limits of the stress performance ratio, consuming excessive amounts of energy, and adding expense to future maintenance requirements.

MEDIAPRO

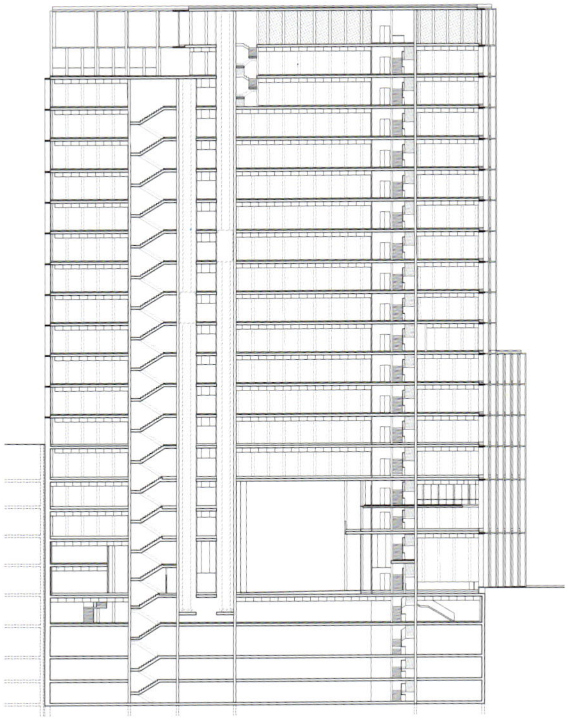

Section

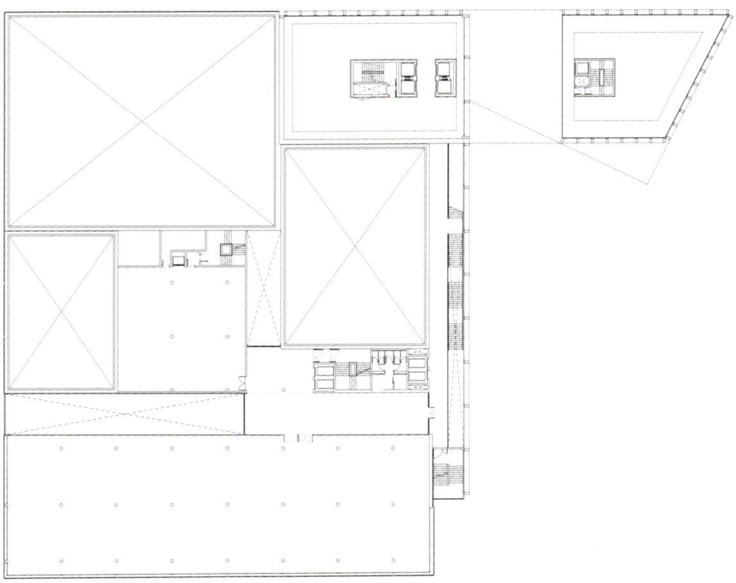

Ground floor plan

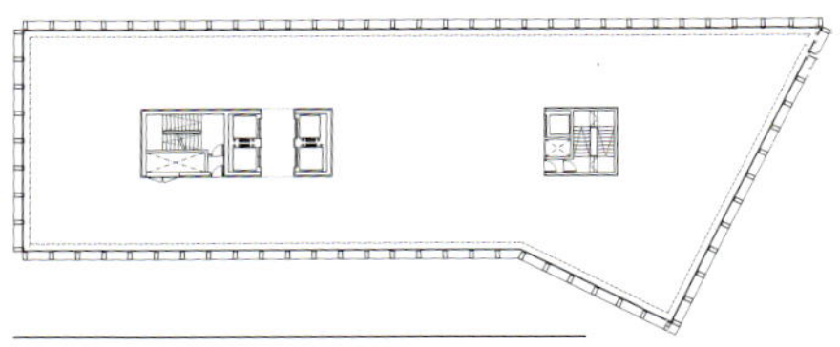

Typical plan of lower floor
with cantilevered overhang

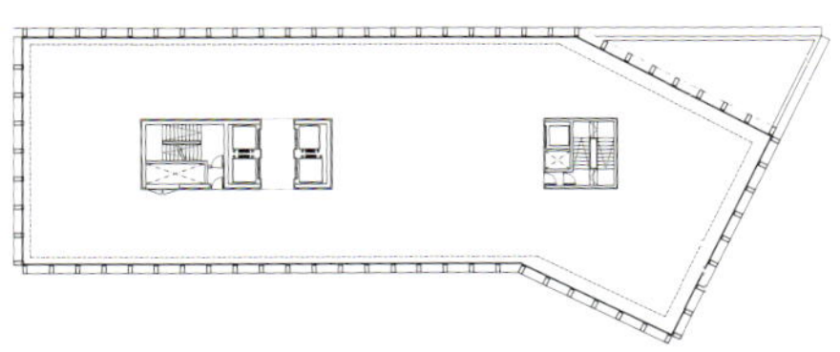

Typical plan of higher floor

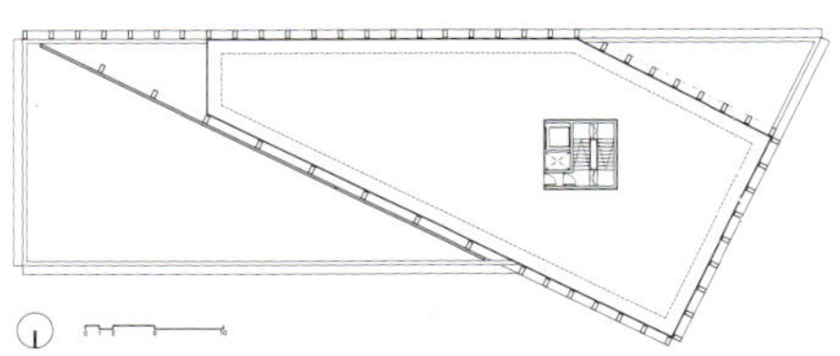

Presidential floor plan

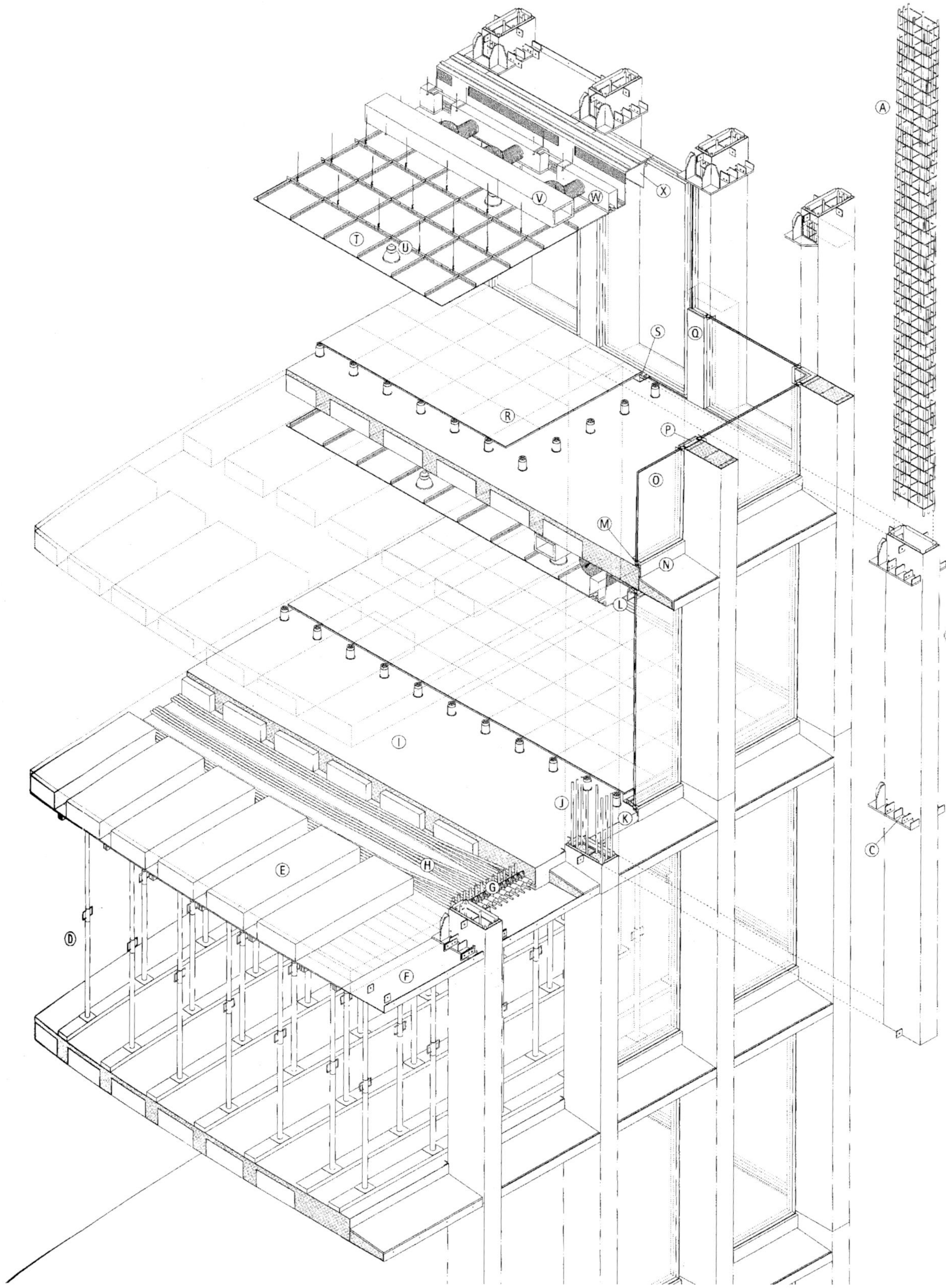

Structure and façade detail. Magazine extract *Tectónica* no.29. Steel (II)

Juan Calvo

Civil engineer for Pondio Engineers

The stretch of Avinguda Diagonal that passes through District 22@—the area of the city being reinvented hand in hand with new technologies—is marked by a sequence of buildings which, with the renowned Agbar Tower as a backdrop, begins with the new headquarters of the Mediapro media group. Given its location, the design of the new building takes into special account the nature of its urban setting, and its volume has been modeled according to alignment and visual sightlines. As a result the main façade has been turned to face the avenue and the first four levels have been perforated to provide an opening for Carrer Bolivia and to direct interest to its perspective. On the lower level, the tower is diverted from the edge of the plot to create a new plane, allowing the adjacent building to be seen.

These operations lend a sculptural feel to the volume, intensified by the cantilevered tower and the resulting arris, and by the horizontal volume with a transparent façade that embraces the new triangular plaza. The office tower's open-plan design provides great flexibility of use due to the absence of pillars and intermediate frames.

The different floors have distinct layouts, permitting a certain functional specialization in their programs that goes beyond the mere separation of the horizontal volume, which housed the audiovisual production and training center, and the tower housing the company's administration.

The versatility of this interior layout is based on the use of a single, repeated window model, developed continuously on all of the façades. These offer good lighting conditions and views of the city from any point of the tower. The glass panes inside the grid prevent glare and are protected from direct sun exposure, water and dirt.

Owing to its perimeter frame, the building's skeleton coincides with its final form. The grid of pillars on the façades and the floor slabs allow it to be considered a large Vierendeel truss, given that the fusion of membranes or structural diaphragms with the post-tensioned slabs make large spans possible and give the structure rigidity. This system means that areas bearing less of the façade load collaborate in withstanding the stress from the more tensioned parts of the grid in a kind of structural democracy. Finally, the greater height of the pillars on the lower levels and at the top—set aside for service installations—and the metallic bronze color used in the structure and window frames give the building the solid and classic air of a great skyscraper.

The building adopts sustainable forms from its urban setting alone, and the natural daylight in all work areas is impeccable. The grid absorbs and spreads daylight uniformly. The structural design was made according to strict environmental criteria. The large glazed expanses giving onto the public plaza are north-facing to avoid excessive exposure to the sun. The roof areas of the lower volume housing the film sets and production areas feature state-of-the-art solar panels.

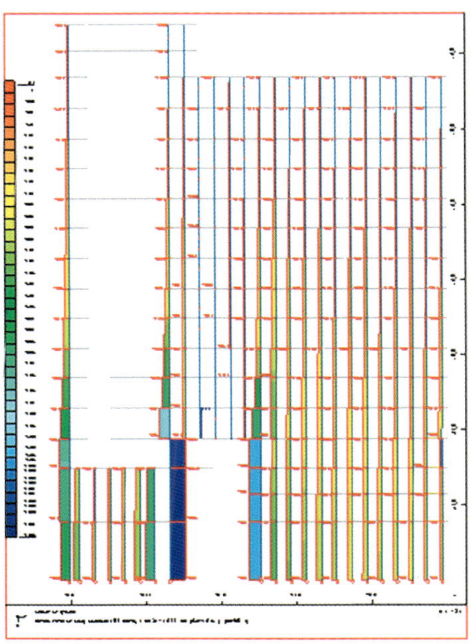

The façade contains 112 different pillar alignments. The perimeter of a standard floor has 74 pillars, separated by 1.90–2.05 m, according to the modular design of each façade. They consist of an outer layer of thick steel plate filled with highly ductile concrete in order to increase their fire-resistance time.

They all have an external perimeter of 60 x 30 cm, with only the thickness of the steel wall varying depending on the load (some of them are of solid steel).

Each post-tensioned floor slab in the tower seems to be "interwoven" from a series of three or four 15 mm-diameter super-stabilized steel cables in a sheath, designed to follow a course made up of straight lines and second-degree parabolas.

The tensioning process commences once the concrete has reached a typical resistance of 200Kp/cm², with a single tensioning stage of 20 Mp.

MEDIAPRO

PLAÇA
GUTENBERG

imagina

RO
ELONA IAGONAL

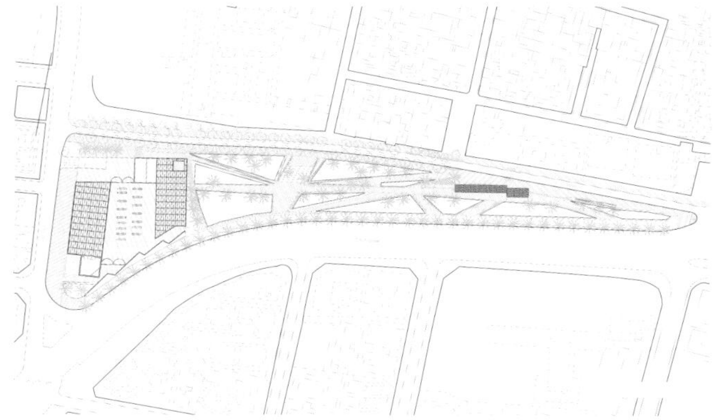

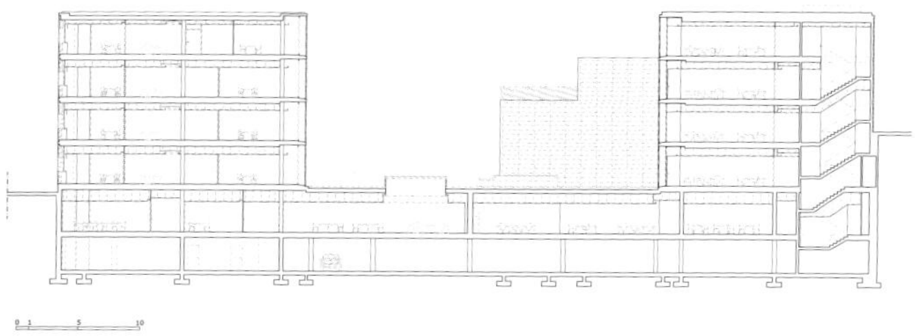

Corporate Headquarters for GISA & FGC

In one of the main entrances to Barcelona, integrated within the operation of covering over the FGC train tracks and the conversion of its former workshops, there appears a rectangular block resulting from the intersection of the urban weaves of the barrios of Sarriá and Tres Torres with Via Augusta, thus generating a huge public space that will function as a hinge to resolve the height difference existing between the two neighborhoods.

Emerging at the intersection of Via Augusta with Carrers Vergós and Cardenal de Sentmenat is the group of buildings of the corporate headquarters of GISA and FGC, which, notwithstanding the restrictiveness of the planning of the specific, pronounced volumetry, stem from a work of urban integration, conferring on them a character typical of institutional buildings, a character at once emblematic, welcoming and functional.

The functional program of the two buildings is resolved by means of diaphanous floors giving onto the public space between them, and of offices in the outer perimeters. The façade modulation is highly refined in order to give flexibility and versatility to the interior distribution. A detailed plan with highly exacting constructional solutions resolves the exterior skin as a whole with a single module of extruded, anodized aluminum.

Roca Barcelona Gallery

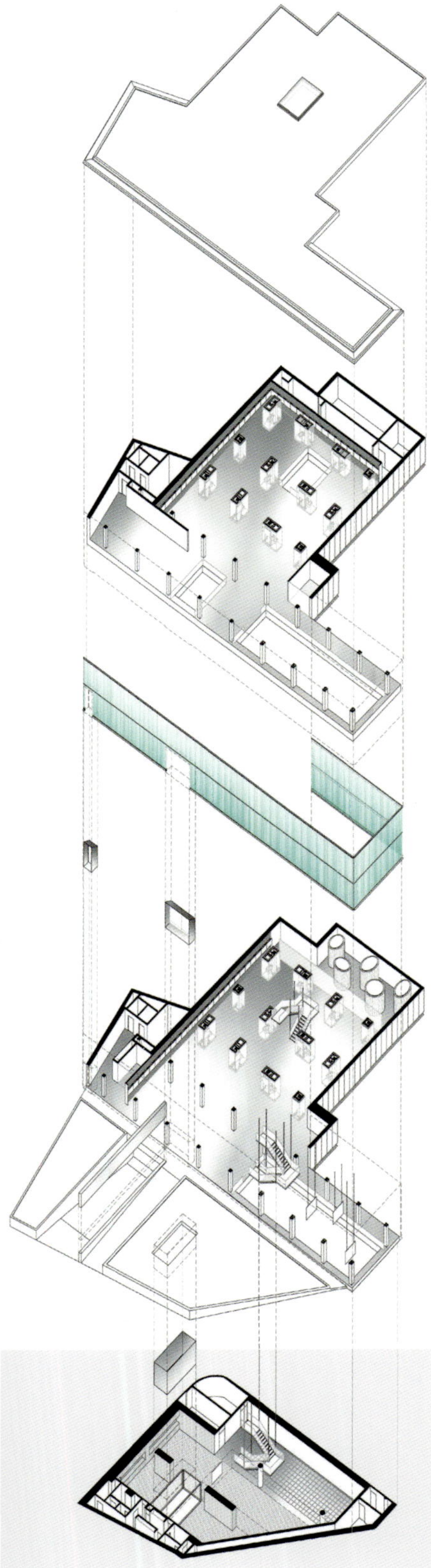

Finally, after considering different opportunities, a solution was reached for the façade, based on the placement of a single material, a succession of multiple panes of glass placed perpendicularly to the axis of the façade. Tests and prototypes were used to confirm how to produce new effects such as diffraction, reflection, and refraction of the light obtained as a result of the distortion, translation and overlaying of images through the façade.

Light, both daylight and artificial nocturnal illumination, became the dominant feature. We achieved a totally ambiguous façade that proved to be an element as solid in the day as it was liquid at night, as heavy as it was light, as rugged as it was smooth, and where it would be difficult at times to know if it was transparent, translucent or opaque. Consequently, when we look in from the outside, the façade offers us an ambiguous and distorted view of the building's interior, making it necessary to enter in order to discover what it is really like inside. Once inside, if we look out towards the city, we observe a series of visual effects, as if it were a game, where nothing is really where it should be. Some rays of light pass through in a straight line, while others are reflected backwards, producing something similar to a superimposed image. At the same time, others are diffracted to show all the colors of the rainbow.

From the inside, we observe streets that were not there before; buildings are doubled, and we see pedestrians walking by and think they are where we see them, while they are actually somewhere else. We fulfilled our aim of a façade that would offer different images of the same reality whenever one looked carefully through it. While designing a building projected towards the exterior, a unique world, space and atmosphere was sought for the interior.

On the inside, light, audiovisual installations, materials, and exhibition elements were used to create an interior that was very different from a typical exhibition space, where the visitor could have an intense and unique experience with the building. Hence, the interior space was designed as a personal and sensory experience in which users or visitors could interact with the building by means of presence detectors, directional loudspeakers, light changes, projections, projected figures, and plasma screens showing objects in movement. All of these elements appear to have been inserted, as if they were floating around an indivisible and continuous space. Slightly reflective and experimental ceramic flooring, a stainless-steel suspended ceiling, and expanded polystyrene foam tetrahedrons on the walls are the three predominant materials featured in the interior.

These are all continuous materials; in the form of three continuous planes they recreate a weightless space, emphasizing horizontality and lacking in spatial or formal references. The physical space becomes a sort of virtual space. The idea of materiality dominates the building. All the materials used—laminated glass on the façade, stainless-steel strips on the ceilings, foam rubber acoustic insulation pyramids and panels set over plywood strips on the walls, and mosaic tiles on the floor—result in multiple joints that can be understood as continuous surfaces owing to the absence of perceptible joins.

We might say typical materials were used yet transformed into new and singular ones. Technology applied to the building, the audiovisuals, and the way of explaining the brand and its products is an essential part of conveying the company's commitment to the future. The Roca Barcelona Gallery project resonates with the most advanced lighting technology. For this Roca and the architectural team at OAB (Borja, Lucía, and Carlos Ferrater) worked together with a team of experts in such different fields as communications, lighting and audiovisuals, and many other specialists who have made it possible to create an original building and an emblem for the brand.

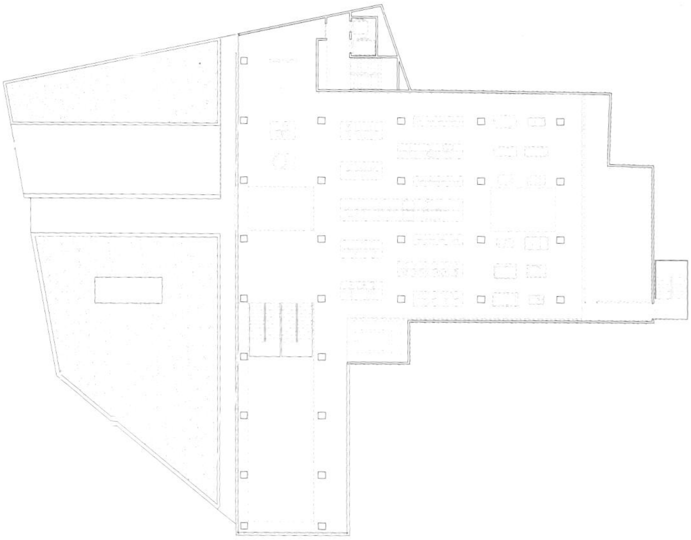

First floor plan

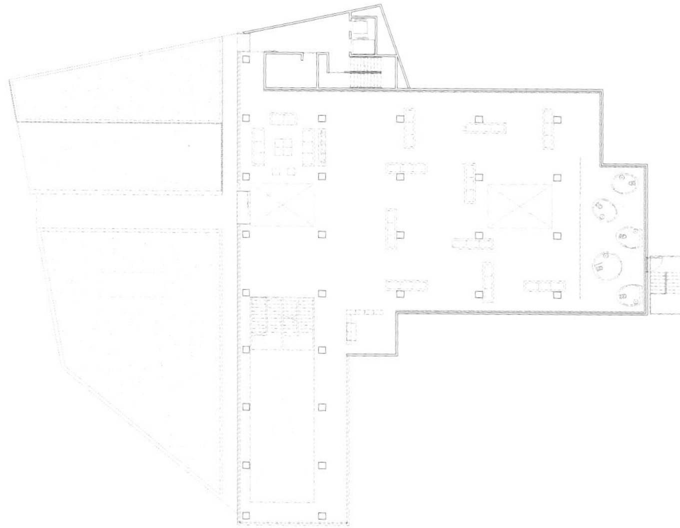

Ground floor plan

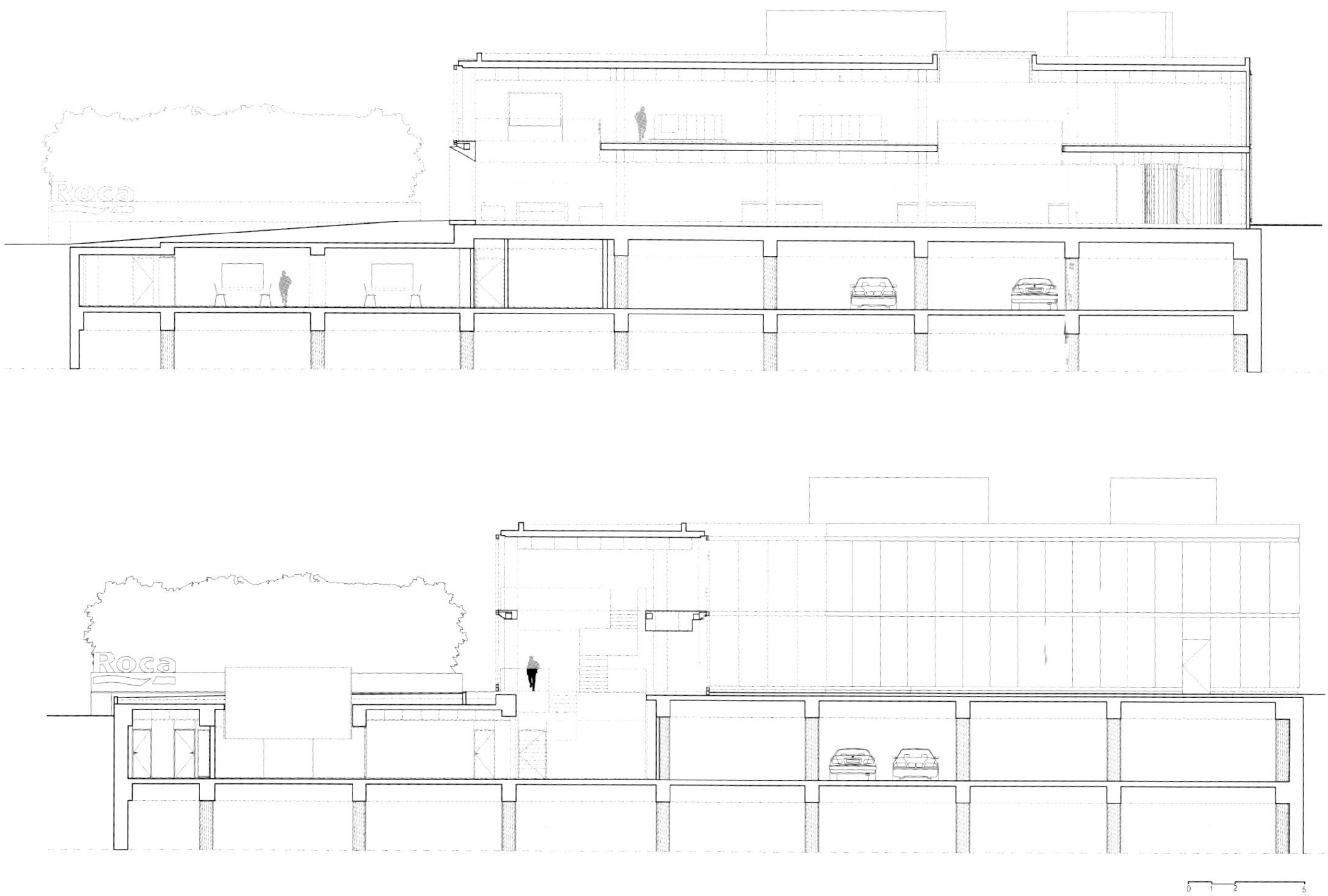

Sections

TAXI
Entrada

Benidorm West Beach Promenade

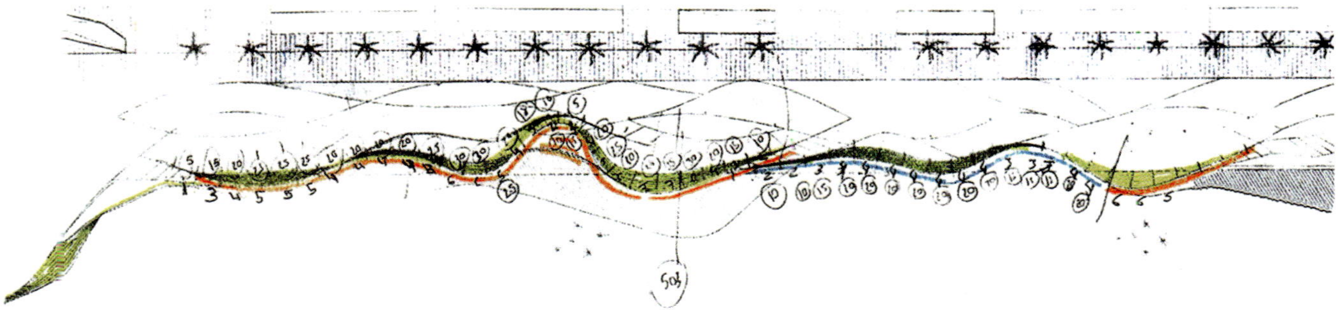

The promenade in Benidorm, a new transitional location between built city and the natural space of sea and beach. The promenade is not understood as a frontier/borderline, but as an intermediary space rendering this transition permeable.

It is structured as a place with a rich topography, as a dynamic space that accommodates the act of strolling and watching the sea, but also organizes different areas for stopping and relaxing in.

The promenade subsumes the longitudinal and transverse flows of the different circulations and channels these, allowing easy access to the beach. It eliminates architectural barriers, permitting direct access from the places for parking.

The promenade thus becomes an architectonic location that molds a new topography and plays with light and shade. A nexus of sinuous interwoven lines which sets up the different spaces and adopts various natural and organic shapes evocative of the fractal structure of a cliff, as well as the motion of waves and tides.

The promenade is structured in different layers: a first structural layer creates the perimeter line in white concrete; another textured layer with paving in different colors; and a last layer of street furniture and natural features like water and vegetation. All these contribute to a homogeneous location with its own personality; as well as being a predecessor to the new architecture of the twenty-first century by combining building technology and nature in one.

The new Benidorm promenade is posited, then, as a new form, one integrating the artificial (or built) and the natural. The project subsumes three different essences within the organic forms of modernism: the forms of fractal geometry in nature; the latest building technologies; and avant-garde landscape design.

The new promenade leaves nothing to chance, but grows out of setting up a number of specific laws, a geometrical ground plan, and modulation. A constructional logic is thus established, facilitating its modulation in sections.

The beach partly invades zones previously occupied by the former esplanade, increasing the surface area of sand and reducing that of asphalt.

All the functional aspects are brought together: the promenade proper, rest and relaxation area, vantage point, transition to the beach, architectural barriers, direct access to parking, rainwater collectors, beach lighting, road communication, integration of street furniture, services infrastructure, and so forth.

A new landside frontage is constructed, providing views of the sea and the beach from the upper level of the promenade, and a new borderline established, integrating the different circulations in its undulations and platforms, eliminating a barrier and constructing a place for people to be in.

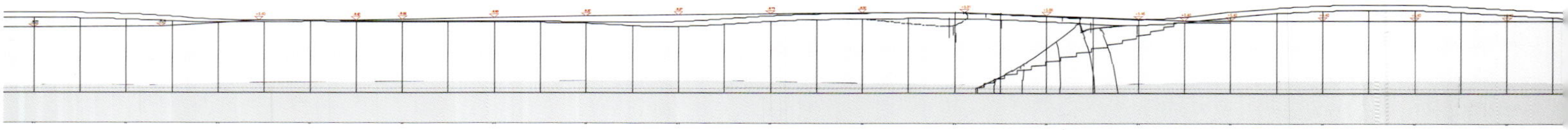

Section

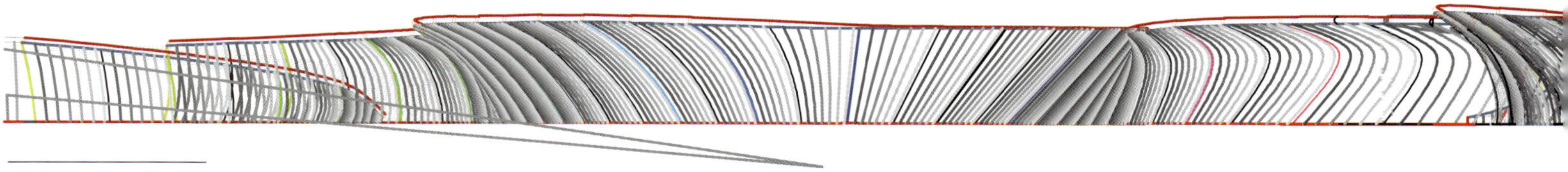

Final elevation

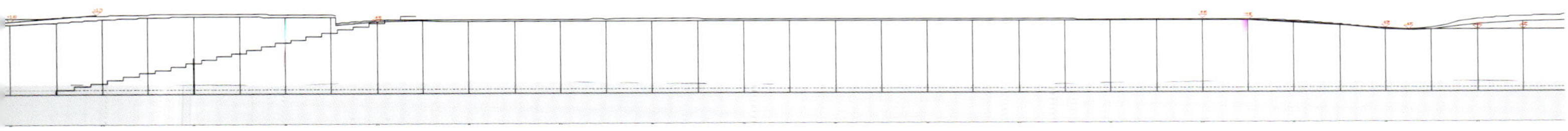

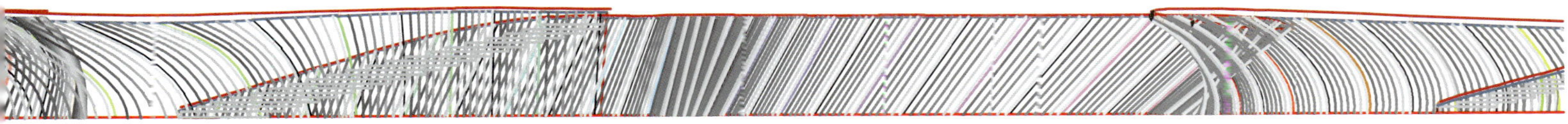

Vegetation plan

108 Social Housing Units

In an enclave close to the city of Barcelona we develop a building with 108 public housing apartments. On the ground floor there is an autonomous commercial space and pedestrian access is via two central communication cores. These cores link the city level with the upper platform level, thanks to an interior pedestrian street which leads to the communal area at the back via patios and landscaped pathways. The volumetric scheme is resolved by means of three seemingly freestanding towers, which go to form the main frontage on the avenue. These are bonded to a slightly lower linear block that acts as a backdrop to the building complex.

The volumes are united in the central empty space by the communication cores. This layout permits all the apartments to be south-facing and with views of the city, and to profit from such eco-efficient passive measures as natural light and cross-ventilation. The three towers emphasize their verticality thanks to their composition. By dematerializing the corners and creating transparency in the foreshortened view, the poetic image of the Miesian skyscraper is evoked. From the point of view of materiality and given the limited budget, there is a studied modulation and a combination of continuous single-layer white facings, with the presence of a noble material like aluminum.

Platform Level

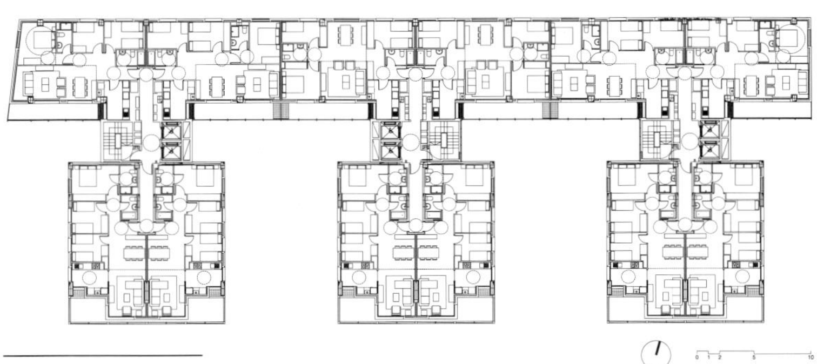

Typical floorl

Vila-real Public Library

Housing and inhabitants

Carlos Ferrater

House for a Photographer 2

A plot perpendicular to the sea measuring 250 m in length by 18 m in width.

The piece of land lies in an agricultural area that runs back from the beach to a place that forms a backdrop of old ruins, reeds and lemon trees.

House for a Photographer 2 stands at the back of the site. Built on a platform raised 50 cm over the floodable natural terrain, three small volumes with irregular layouts and elevations create a dialogue through a void with visual distractions.

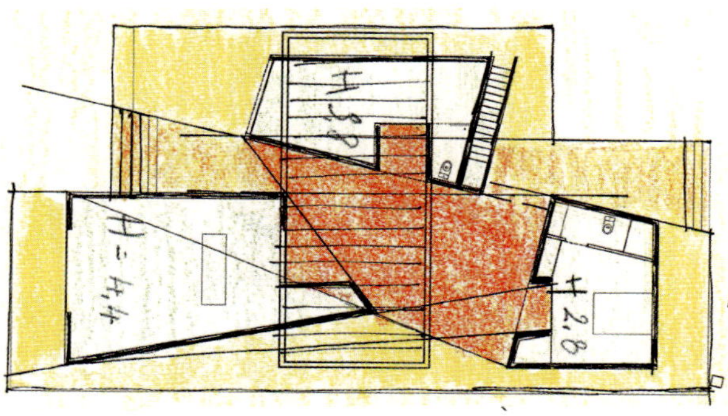

La fàbrica d'Horta
(Factory in Horta), 1909
Pablo Picasso

A grove of 51 Washingtonia palms leads from the beach to the house.
The deconstructed volumes adapt to the conditions of the landscape, of buildings and light that suggest a painting by Picasso that was painted in the area and now hangs in the Picasso Museum in Paris.

The central void becomes the main space of the house, a tense space geometrically composed in its upper part through the tall, opaque structures of the different pavilions, and from the ground up to a height of 2.10 m on a continuous site where the different shaded interior spaces are connected with views of the sea, the lush backdrop, and the living areas on the platform.

The set of deconstructed volumes reminds us of Picasso's Cubist work.
The chiaroscuro and the intense light of this area of the Mediterranean balance the flat landscape of this part of the Ebro Delta.

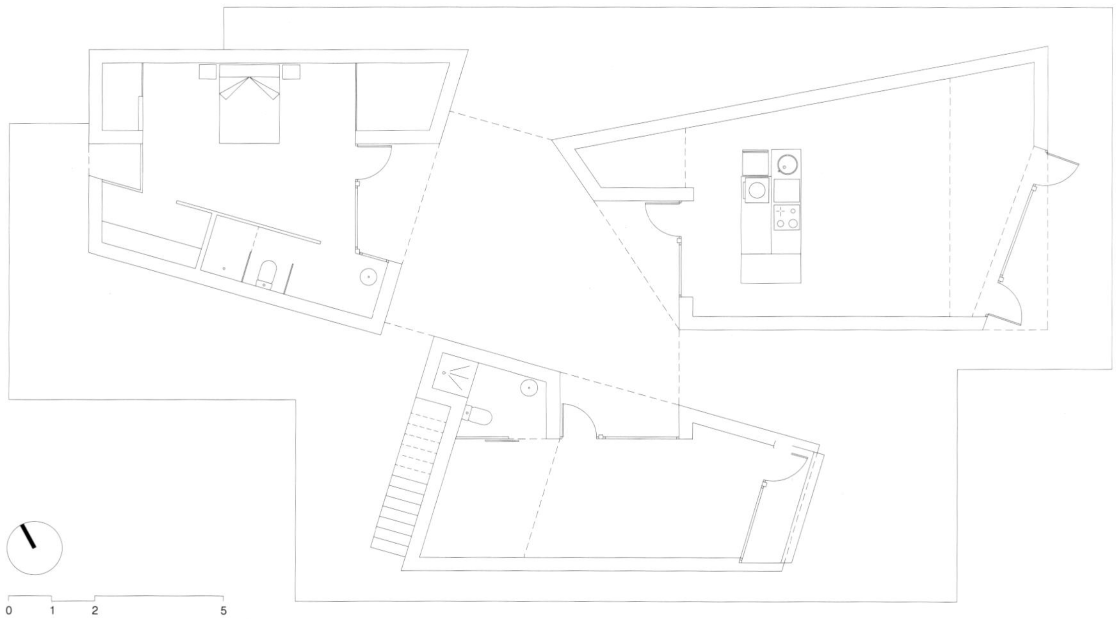

Floor plan

Section

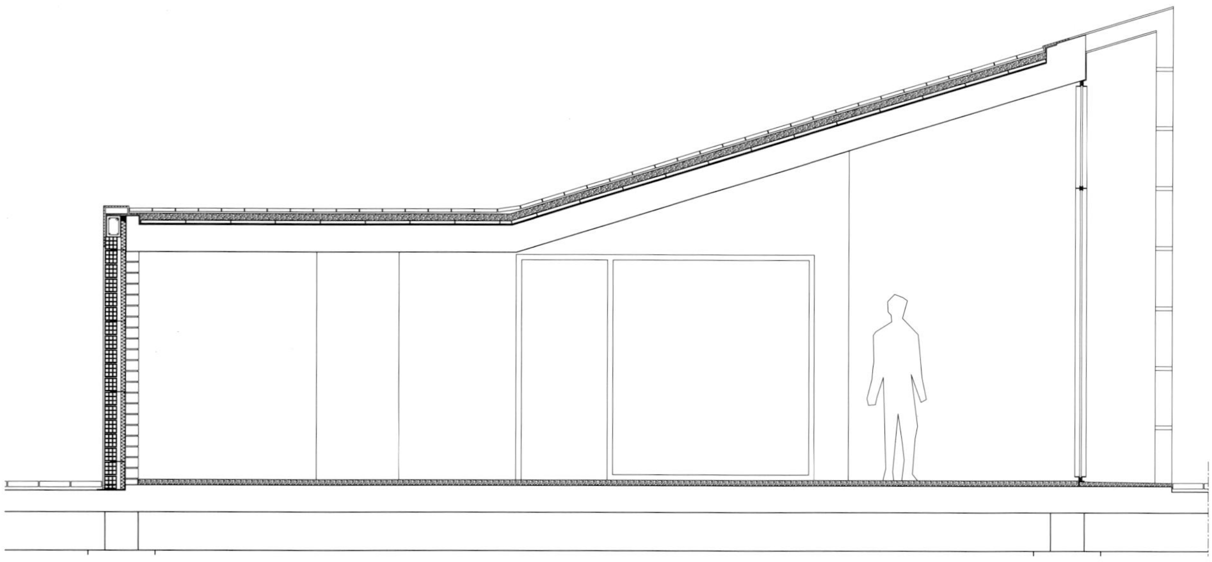

Construction section

AA House is not one house; it is four

AA House by Carlos Ferrater and Xavier Martí is one of the most unique and intense single-family homes that has been built in recent times. It establishes a relationship with houses by Louis Khan, Alison and Peter Smithson, and Ray and Charles Eames.

Located in Sant Cugat, beside a forest bordering a golf course, the house rises from the road as a series of sloping roofs among the trees in the garden that form a magnificent belt of picturesque scenery.

On entering, the house greets us with a pool of water, an allegory of one of the four elements and born of a desire for reflections. Before entering, a totally austere piazza is defined. And upon entering, you discover a great longitudinal space, defined by skylights in the sloping roof. This great interior space is at once on a perfect human scale.

The unique and unsettling fact that there appears to be no staircase, and that none of the service facilities of the house are visible, all hidden away on a lower floor, leads us to believe this is not a house but something else; it is many houses at one and the same time. It is more of a pavilion than a house, given that the only thing to emerge is a large open level of rectangular panels in a bright white, like a temporary Japanese pavilion or a marquee. The house is surrounded by grass, as if it were itself a form of plant life, and floats above it, taking on a mythical and imaginary image. It is reminiscent of the volumes of La Ricarda, the house by Antoni Bonet Castellana.

From the inside it becomes, rather than a house to stay in, a large chamber. This sensation owes much to the orthogonal floor plan, perceived as diagonality and dynamicity; the cross-section develops into inclined volumes capturing views of the landscaped garden and of the distant landscape beyond, incorporated into the landscape surrounding the house.

In short, it is more than a house, or even a pavilion or a chamber; it is like a boat anchored in a green sea of grass. The stairs of this boat are what reveal this secret quality, hidden inside this light and airy house, which seems to be on the point of floating away. The four staircases leading to the lower domains are always hidden and always narrow, like those on a boat. A staircase beside the dining room and kitchen leads directly to the basement. There is a narrow staircase in the bedroom, which, also styled like those on a boat, leads between the walls directly down to the indoor swimming pool and sauna. A light and modern staircase goes from the library directly down to the cinema room, the space for fantasy and dreaming. Finally, there are service stairs leading down from the entrance, next to the kitchen, to the domestic staff apartment.

There are other stairs, also an important feature and, likewise, in the style of a boat, that go up to the higher levels, such as the lightweight contraption that unfolds like a ladder in the library and leads up to a loft where the owner's map collection is kept, the observatory of the world. The kitchen is another house, a world opening onto the garden and bathed in natural daylight, a systematic laboratory of nutrition, care, cleaning, and work.

It is then that we discover the fourth house, which is the hidden house, the collector's house. It belongs to the collector of cars that are stored in the garage on the lower level. While the visible and representative house, after entering, next to the bar, is the large light-filled living area with piano and library at the back, the truly structuring space, the most private inner sanctum of the house, is not visible. It is the large garage belonging to the collector, where the permanent occupants of the house are to be found: cars, like machines of the subconscious, of desire, and of speed.

It is a house and it is the opposite of a house—telluric and anchored at the base, and yet light and floating like a balloon about to leave the ground. It takes us back to the idea of a "house" as an authentic archetype, as understood by Gaston Bachelard and Luís Barragán: with a basement and an attic. With all of its intensity and meaning, this house contains all the symbols. It is a house on pleasant land, all garden, which floats above the grass.

It is not a house. It is many houses. This is what makes it so unique, mythical, archetypal and unsettling. It is a world of illusions: it is a pavilion that floats on a green sea; it is a large chamber to capture the surroundings in a thousand ways; it is a boat moored to the trees; it is a balloon about to take to the sky, anchored to the ground by a basement full of machines. it is, in short, the secret world dreamed of by two collectors.

West elevation

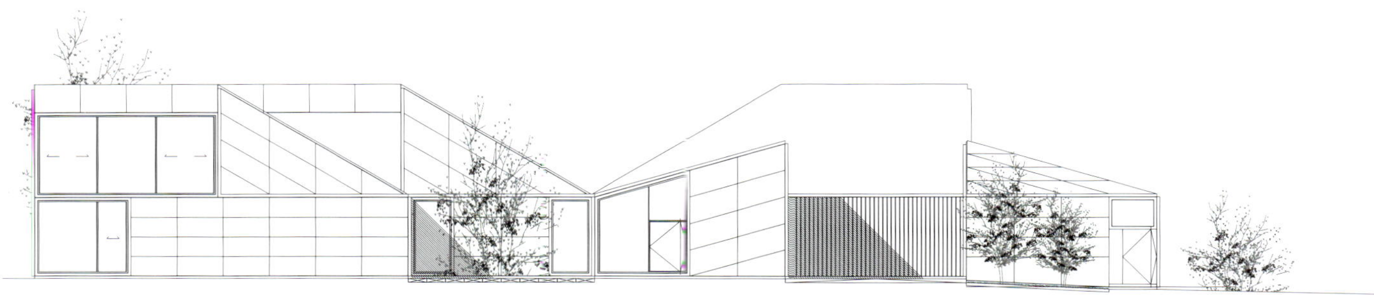

East elevation

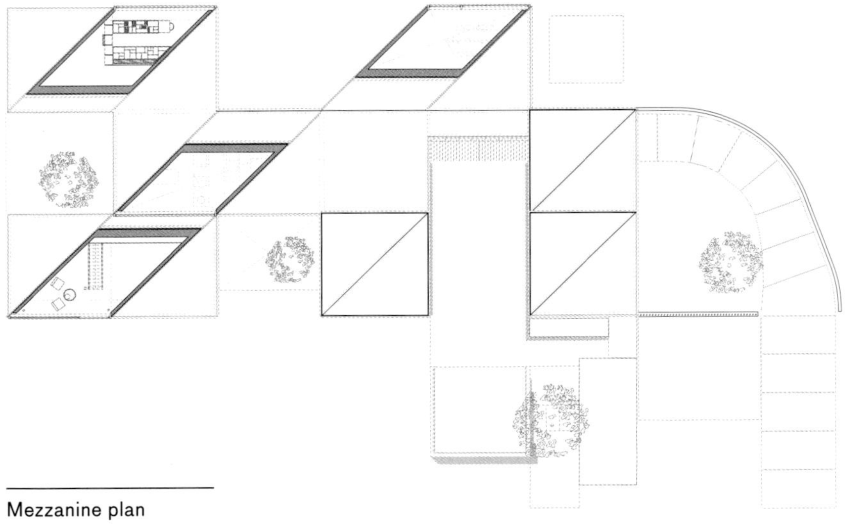

Mezzanine plan

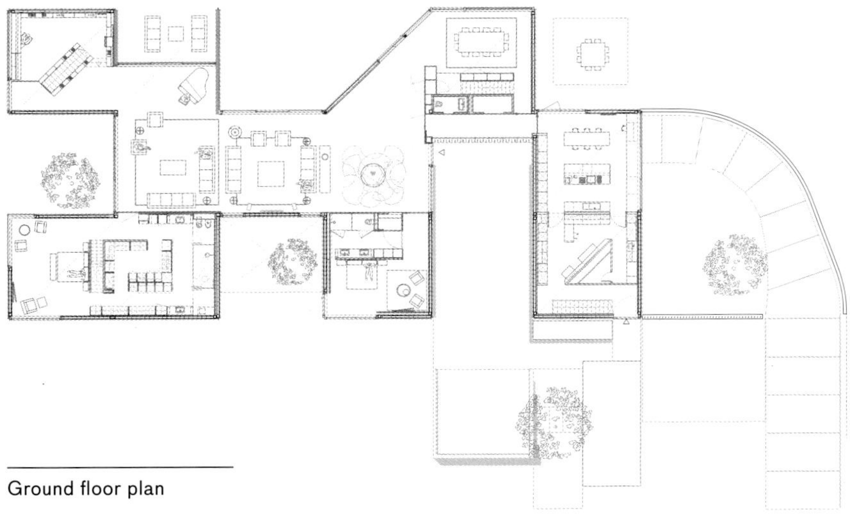

Ground floor plan

Basement floor plan

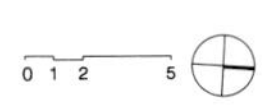

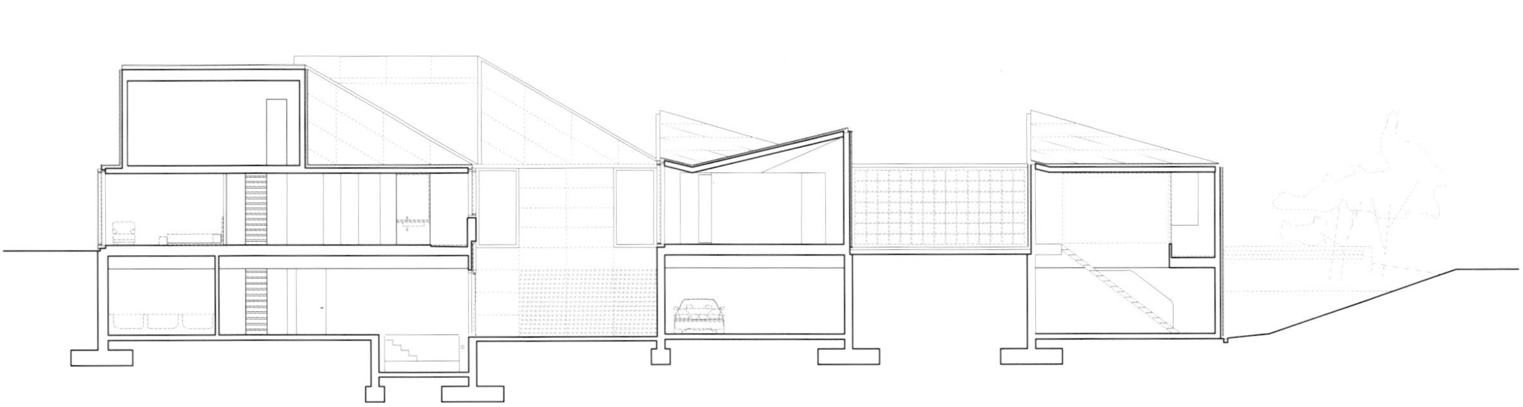

Longitudinal section

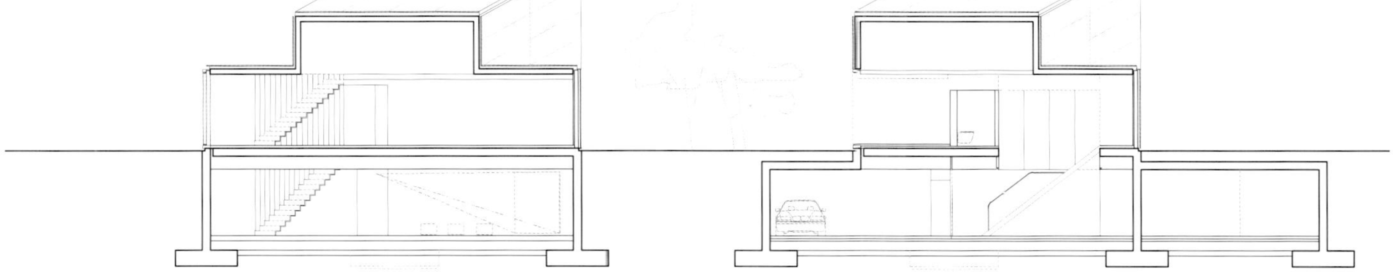

Cross section

BF House

This house is on a 3,000 m^2 plot with a height difference of 25 m, in a Castellón neighborhood. Looking at the plot, we can see that it bears the mark of its seventeenth-century history, which is when overpopulation led to the cultivation of all types of terrain, including those that are very steep, via a system of small terraces with walls made of local rock. Our position vis-à-vis the plot of land was one of absolute respect; therefore, the construction method was also intended to respect the land. As a result we opted for a prefabricated building system that sits upon the ground almost without touching it, without cutting down trees, and by taking advantage of existing terrace/garden areas.

Part of the house—the garage and the auxiliary areas—is buried, allowing us to reintroduce native vegetation on the natural terrain. In terms of construction, in trying to lessen the impact on the ground we chose a metal structure fabricated in a workshop and transported to the site in large pieces that could be assembled.

An existing stone terrace supports the back part of the structure. This house looks as though it is suspended or in flight due to the dry construction materials used. The façade, resulting in various layers, is finished on the outside with corrugated sheet metal, specially designed to prevent glare and heat thanks to the shadows caused by the folds. The great front opening is oriented towards magnificent views, and allows adequate sunlight in during the winter, but also protects from the sun in the summer. The solar energy panels with heat pipe technology on the roof guarantee that there will always be hot water available for both domestic use and under-floor heating.

Taking advantage of the different orientations, air currents cross the patio, thus permitting a reduction in air-conditioning consumption. The intermediate courtyard permits access under the house, and at the same time allows all the rooms to face the sun and the views. The whole house revolves around this courtyard.

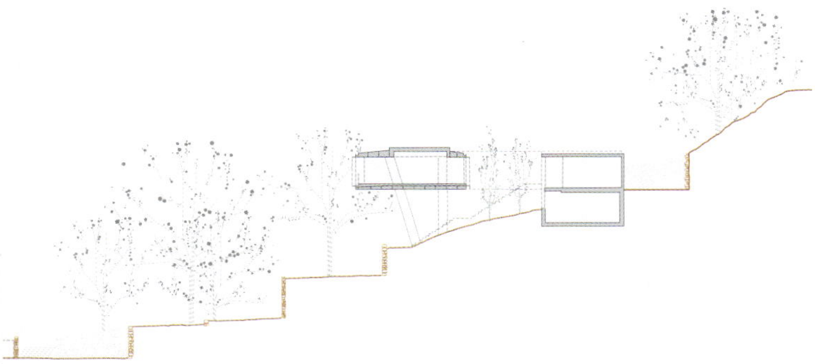

Cross section

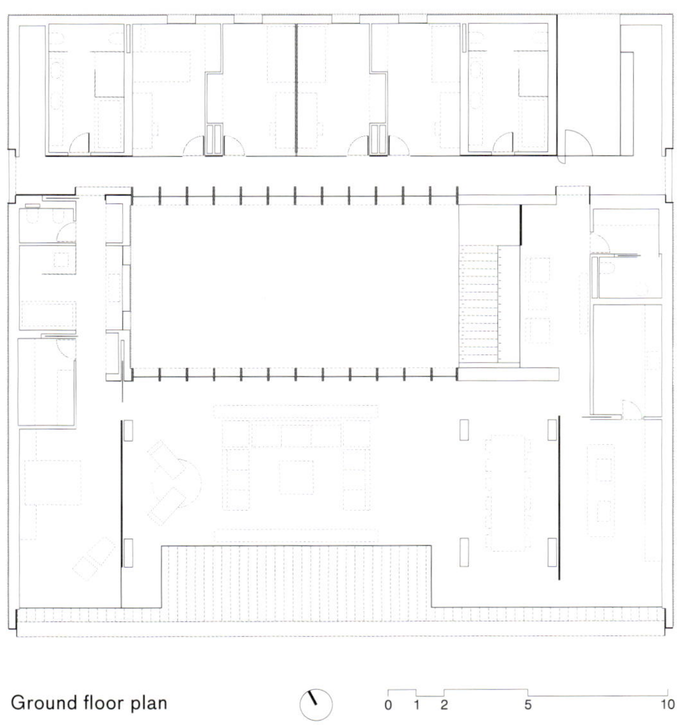

Ground floor plan

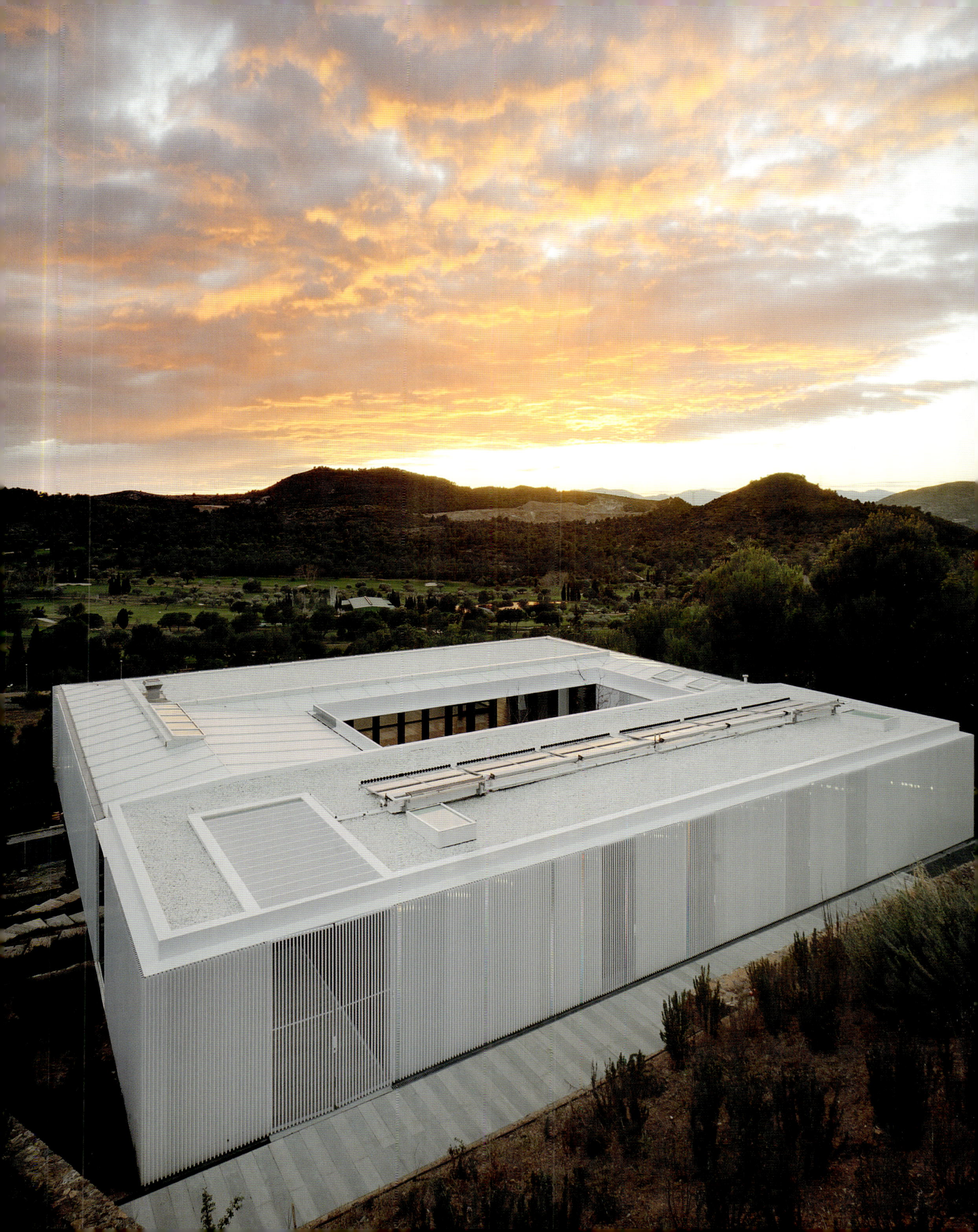

Refurbishment of my parents' house in L'Escala

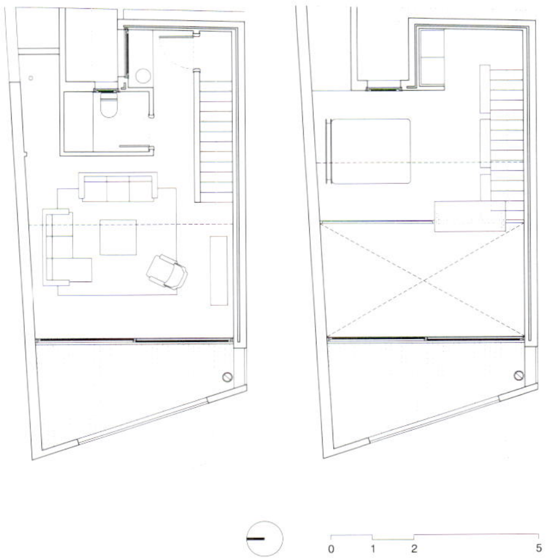

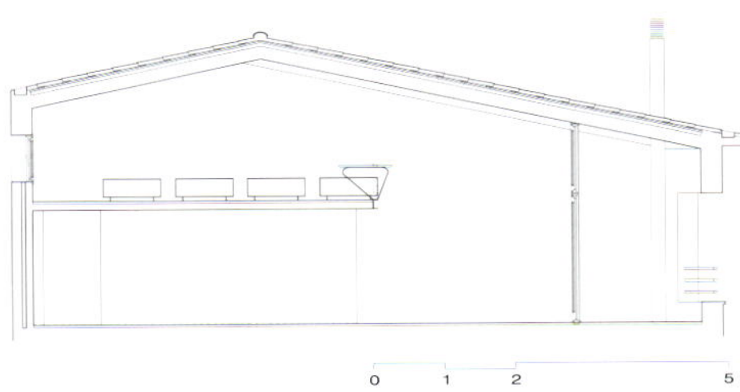

The refurbishment of the little party-wall house, built for my parents in 1960, is carried out by treating it programmatically as an extension of the house rehabilitated in 2012 or as an independent weekend unit. A single space with a sleeping platform, making good use of the height afforded by the section and the inclination of the roof, accommodates a small lounge-cum-dining room with an office space and bathroom, thus permitting its use as an independent entity within the house.

Due to the geometry of the land lot, the tiled roof, as laid down in the planning regulations, was moved back in order to permit the edge to be horizontal. The real window consists of the great sheet of glass recessed towards the interior, thus constructing the small intermediary space of a terrace, and letting a perforation in the façade wall frame the eastward view over the Gulf of Roses. When seated within, the glass profile of the freestanding handrail coincides with the line of the horizon and the long curtains give something of a theatrical touch to the landscape they frame.

Cluster in Kaplankaya, Turkey

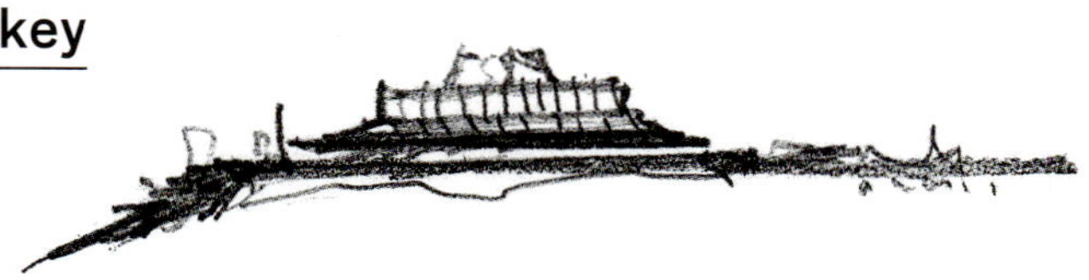

In the eastern Mediterranean, on the west coast of Turkey, facing the Greek islands, close to Bodrum, the ancient Halicarnassus, atop a headland 135 m above sea level, the new building is constructed in keeping with the fortresses, citadels, churches, and monasteries that have characterized the landscape of the Mediterranean.
A banked wall of stone from the immediate vicinity delimits the geometric ground plan and the grounds themselves, helping the upper horizontal plane of the platform to merge with the natural topography, illuminated by patios and fissures in the wall, the complementary program of hammam, gymnasium, and accesses to the upper platform.

Upon this platform, on a 40 x 40 meter-square ground plan with its axis on a north-south diagonal (the orientation of the Blue Mosque in Istanbul), there is a structure of screens, cantilevered girders, and concrete pillars that go to form the skeleton of the building. A huge 6 m eave protects the ground-floor level beneath its shade, acting as a porch and intermediary space between inside and outside. On it, an intercolumniation of screens and pillars, along with huge roof lanterns, rounds the building off against the sky.

Within, an ample, off-center, double-height atrium is converted into the heart of the building: a place for exhibitions, encounters and celebrations. The different interiors—dining room, hall, library, cinema, assembly rooms—wrap around the great atrium on the ground floor, as, on the upper floor, do the apartments and the offices that complete the program. From this level, an open courtyard affords access to the upper viewing terrace. The flexibility of its structure will have to enable different uses and demands to be accommodated over the course of time. In its conception the intervention seeks after timelessness and permanence.

First floor plan

Ground floor plan

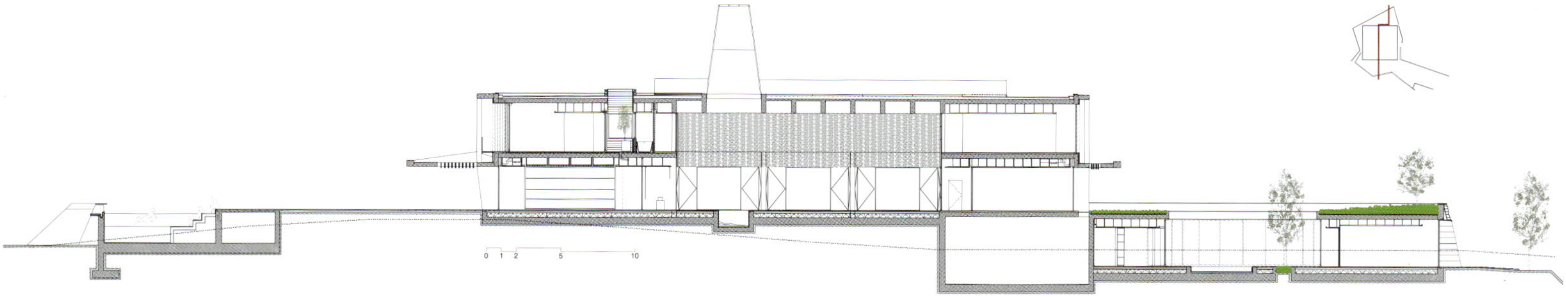

Section

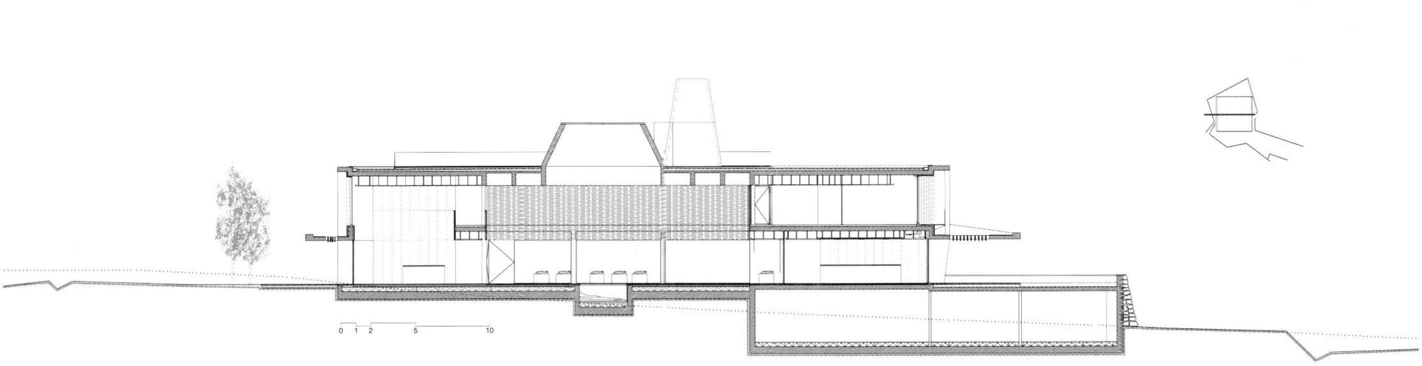
0 1 2 5 10

Milky way July 8th, 2013

Drone Photo March 2015

In Progress

With the creation of Office of Architecture in Barcelona in 2005 the studio embarked on a new phase, a decade-long phase which has produced the projects and built works featured in this monograph.

In 2007 Spain was hit by a severe economic crisis, from which it is still suffering. During the course of those years, and on the basis of having constructed a number of buildings outside the country, buildings like the Michelin Gastronomy Group Head Office in Paris or the Aquileia Tower and public space in the middle of the Lido di Jesolo in Venice, we were able to win our first commission in Turkey, the Kaplankaya Cluster, now completed, a project that has opened up a range of possibilities for us to work in other locations and other cities. So it is that we are currently constructing, also in Turkey, a large hotel integrated into the landscape on the coast at Bodrum, the ancient Halicarnassus, while for the same company we have designed a complex mixed-use building in the Design District in Miami city center, which we present in this monograph.

During the last few years OAB has had, after winning a competition, the chance to build the headquarters of the NGO Fundació Catalana de l'Esplai, thus opening the door to a non-profit collaboration aimed at building summer camps for kids in various parts of Catalonia, like the one now completed in Viladoms, at the foot of the Montserrat mountain range, or others under construction in the old rectory and church in Navés and in Sant Joan de les Abadesses in the pre-Pyrenees.

Similarly, the accolades and the prizes for the Promenade in Benidorm have permitted us to undertake seafront projects in various cities, an example being the one we executed in Tangier in Morocco, with the conversion of the old port and the Corniche which runs around the bay, or the scheme for the waterfront in the town of Niterói in Rio de Janeiro, Brazil.

Over that same decade OAB has made an impact in an area the studio has much experience of, namely urban-minded buildings that are firmly implanted in the city, such as the Law Society in Lyon, a recent competition win; the office block in Guadalajara, Mexico; the hotel facing Santa Caterina Market in the old part of Barcelona; and the city's new fish market, together with the old harbor mouth lighthouse, today's Clock Tower on the fisherman's wharf.

Also to do with the port of Barcelona, and in collaboration with Barcelona Regional, our studio is currently working on plans for a new maritime barrio and garden on top of and beneath the Ronda Litoral as a hinge between city and port; a project that embraces an old studio aspiration: "horizonscrapers," buildings with various uses, literally driven into the cliff of Montjuïc, that stick out over the Ronda and the port. The project incorporates the scheme for an elevator system that would connect the sea-level elevation with the Miramar road and the approaches to the old beacon, and the castle on the upper reaches of the mountain. All these are projects which allow us to continue working tenaciously on our city.

Accordingly, the final chapter of this monograph describes a group of projects that reflect OAB's recent studio work, projects which bear witness to the input of Núria Ayala and the young architects Anna Piqué, Montserrat Trilla and Ignasi Gutiérrez, along with other collaborators who have participated during the last three years in the design process and creative development of our studio.

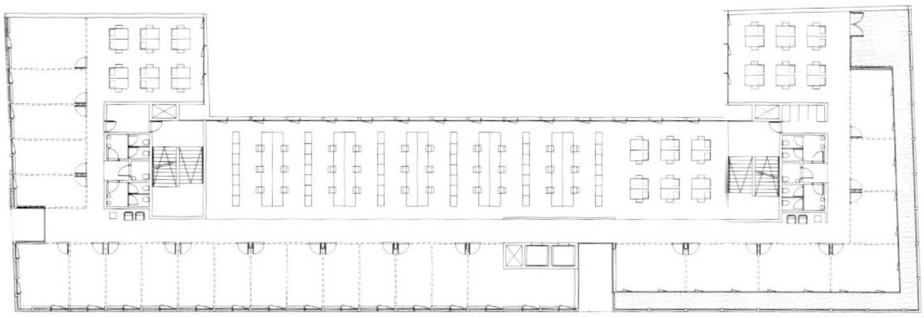

Lawyers Offices level

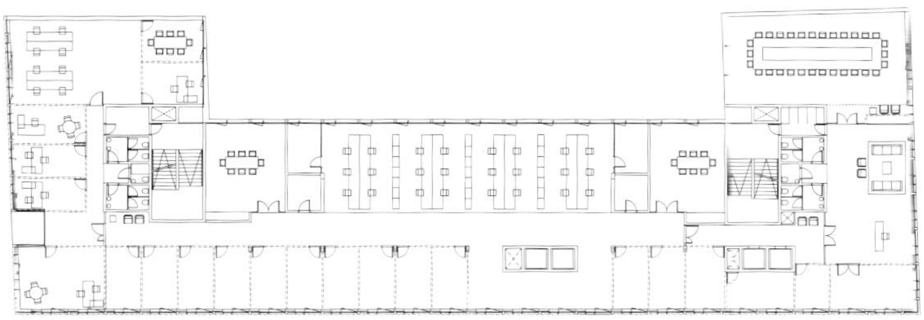

Law Society level

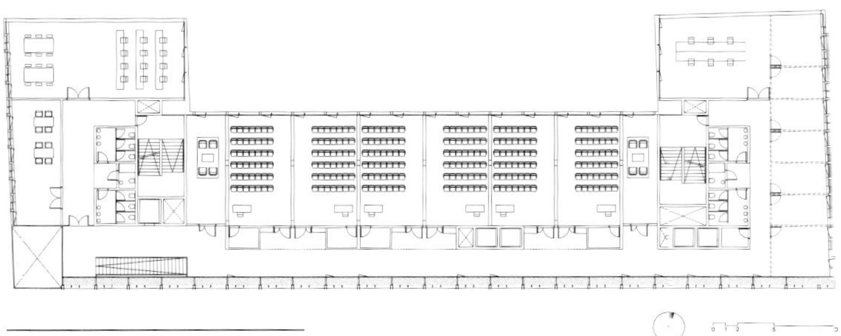

Lawyers School level

Law Society in Lyon France

In the city of Lyon, Rue Servient has an urban potential that makes the former district archive building lot particularly interesting, connecting the Place des Jacobins, Wilson Bridge and Part-Dieu railway station. Its contiguity with the court district and different public transport systems, and its proximity to the *mairie* of the 3eme arrondissement, make of this site a relevant spot on the left bank of the River Rhône.

The first decision in the project was to enhance that multiplicity while responding to a highly contemporary mixed program: three main uses that will reveal themselves to the city while preserving the unity of the intervention. It is therefore an operation for urban integration that also attempts to reconstruct the unitary appearance of the district block.

The project chooses to avoid the opacity of some official buildings and, convinced of a certain political and democratic condition of architecture, privileges the transparency of its activities.
A private building, then, but one with a public and institutional character that reveals its circulations and its programmatic horizontal division, and which becomes porous and accessible from the public space.

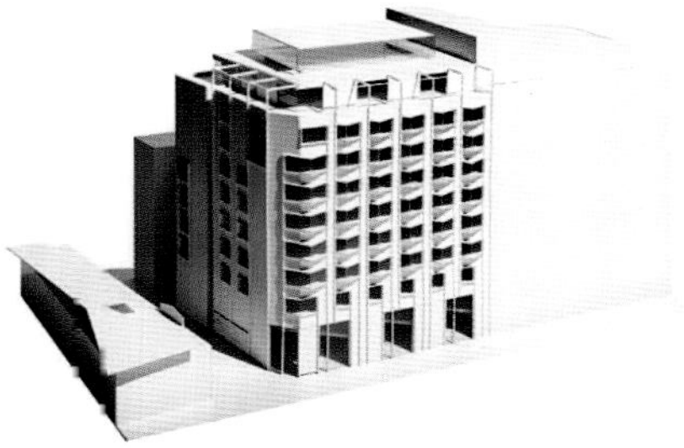

Hotel in Avinguda Francesc Cambó Barcelona

The new building overlooking Avinguda Francesc Cambó, in line with the Cathedral axis, the Santa Caterina Market, and a narrow street in the old town, will be built over an exist building.

With its transformation into a hotel, each façade responds to the varied orientations and urban requirements, and the different planes are unified by large black granite slabs which reflect the market rooftops on the north façade.

A central axis articulates the plan and contains the patios, service cores, staircases and elevators, technical rooms, etcetera, while the hotel rooms are distributed on the perimeter and the preferential corner is reserved for the larger suites.

Level 8 floor plan

RECEPTION LEVEL

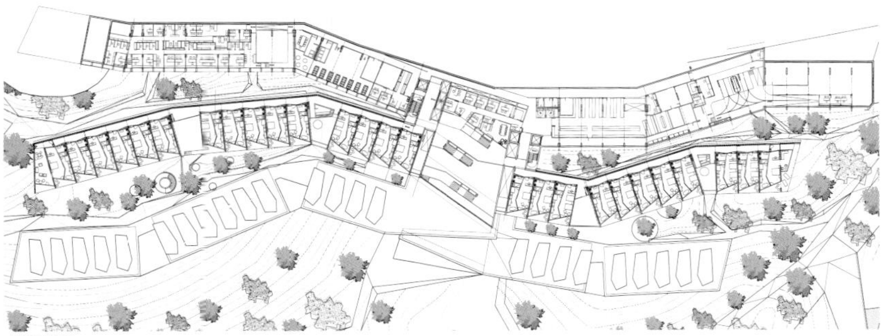

BACK OF HOUSE LEVEL

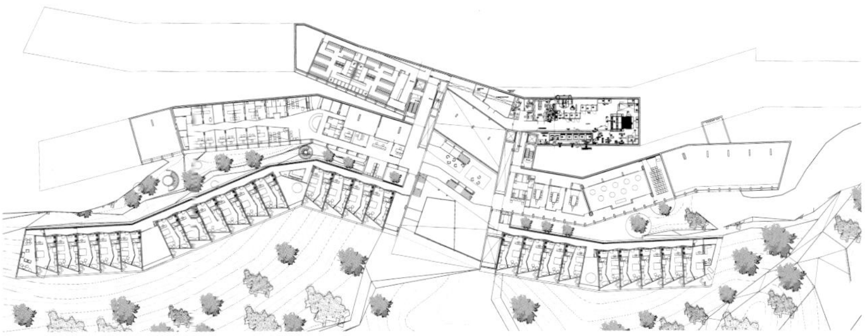

FACILITIES LEVEL

SPA LEVEL

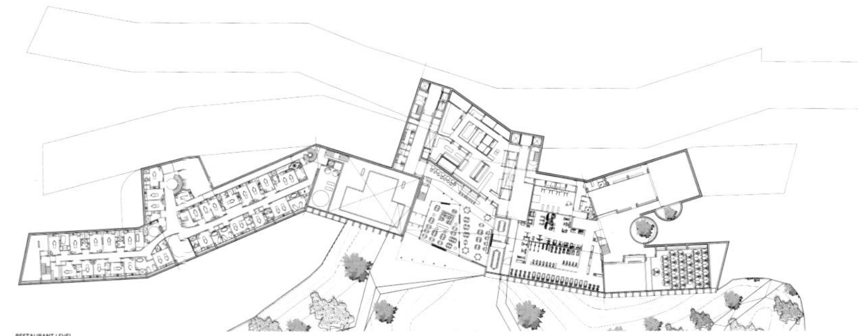

RESTAURANT LEVEL

Canyon Ranch Hotel in Bodrum Turkey

We are not trying to urbanize a mountain, but to build a place for people. Arrive, leave, and return—that will be the condition of this new place. An identity based on a relationship with nature. Utilizing similar rules for different units of activity—streets, piazzas, houses, landscape—and taking advantage of the fractal geometric conditions of the landscape, new natural forms related to the Mediterranean paradigm appear.

The different buildings are finding accommodation in the topography; so many corners of the landscape become viewpoints from which to relate to the sea, sky and vegetation in an atmosphere of privacy and relaxation. The hotel is situated in a privileged position. This facilitates the accessibility and logistics, as well as the optimal relation with the bungalows and rental villas that will complete the hotel. This privilege is most evident in its proximity to the sea and beaches.

The hotel is built on a new typology that hasn't existed to date. A configuration that, from the center outwards, allows the functional program to be organized and articulated by opened and closed spaces in the form of branches. These adapt to the topography and create gaps that promote privacy, light, and quality views, ambience and landscape. Thus, Kaplankaya Canyon Ranch Ridge Community recreates the imagery of the great resort, the underlying idea of the spa, and the romantic spirit of the great hotels of history, linked to Landscape.

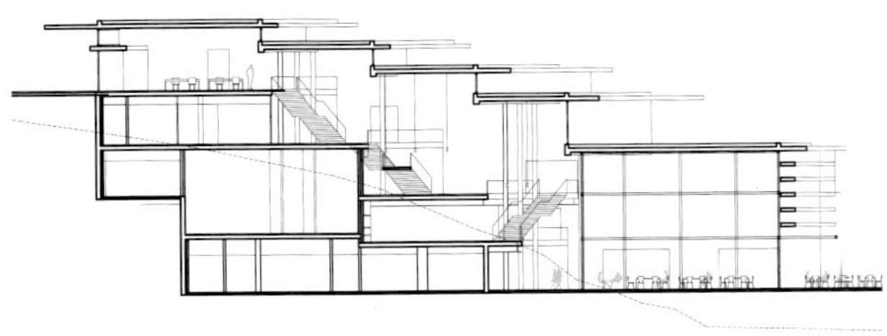

Hotel Section

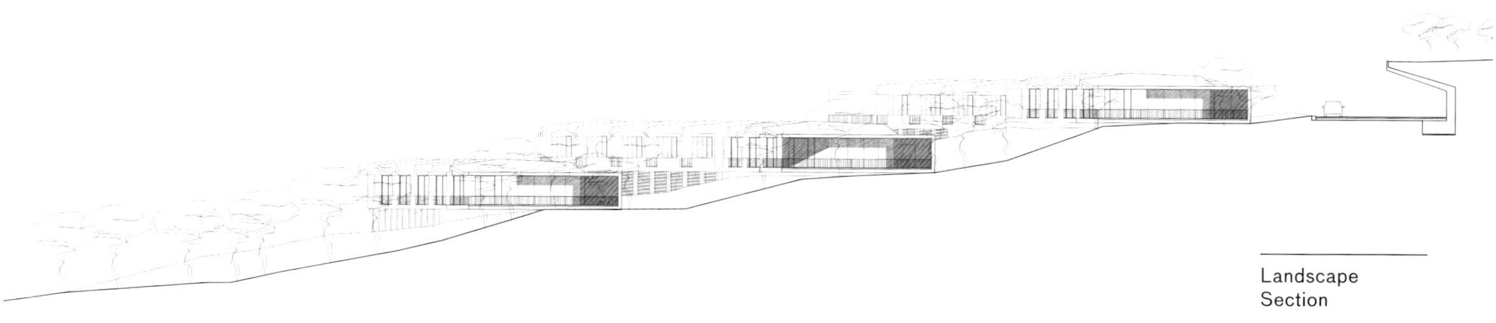

Landscape
Section

Office Building in Guadalajara Mexico

The tower is located on Avenida de la Patria, near the intersection with Avenida de las Américas, on an irregular site at a different street level with respect to Calle Hipódromo de Zapopán.

The project adapts the tower floor plan to the geometry of the plot, formally responding to the urban conditions of the site—namely, the nearby buildings and the façade facing the avenue—until it forms a slim volume, complex in both plan and height, with a distinct crown outlined against the sky.

The circulation and services core is centered and placed at the back of the site, articulating the two office areas on each floor. The tower emerges from the ground over a concrete base that adapts to the irregular geometry of the site, while the parking levels are resolved with sloping slabs that descend helicoidally, with the parking spaces placed on the perimeter. The building's modular envelope, formed by the structural concrete grid, has a double façade: the interior glazing, which provides the openings necessary for maintenance and ventilation, and the exterior one, composed of a thick square lattice built with glass-reinforced concrete that adapts to the structural grid openings.

Cross Section

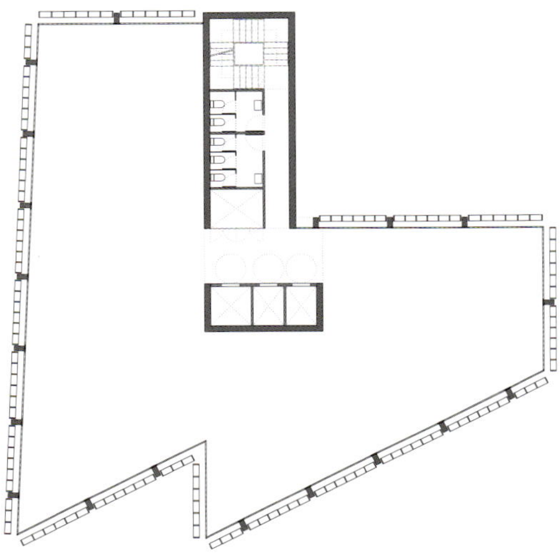

Levels 1-7

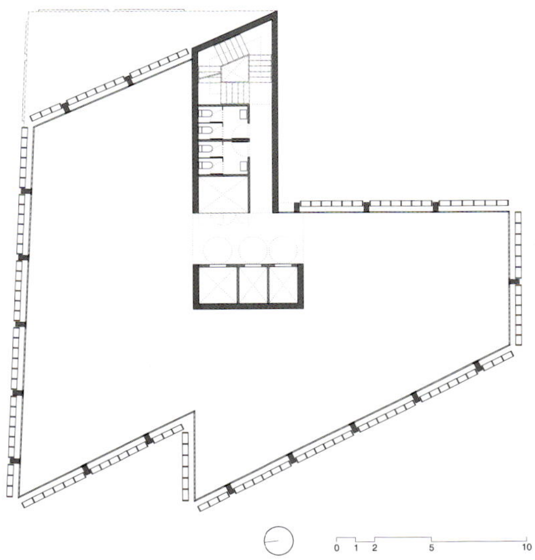

Levels 8-13

Tangier Waterfront

Morocco

The project for Tangier's Corniche brings together certain concepts tried and tested by OAB in two previous projects, the Barcelona Botanical Garden with its grid of pathways, reinforced earth walls, and vegetation communities in a maritime climate, and the cantilevers in the Benidorm seafront promenade, a topography which unfolds between the city and the sea with ceramic pavements and colors typical of the place, and furniture elements and native vegetation that complete the intervention.

The new "corniche promenade" in Tangier provides a backbone for the seaside districts, residential areas and popular sport facilities, preserving the natural conditions of the maritime geography. The solution for the new marina and leisure port is completed with the *plaisance* buildings: bars, restaurants, sailing clubs and leisure zones. The berth borders are detached and floating in order to preserve the public use of the water while at the same time addressing the tide issue. The buildings on the marina dock are built with lightweight concrete structures and lattices.

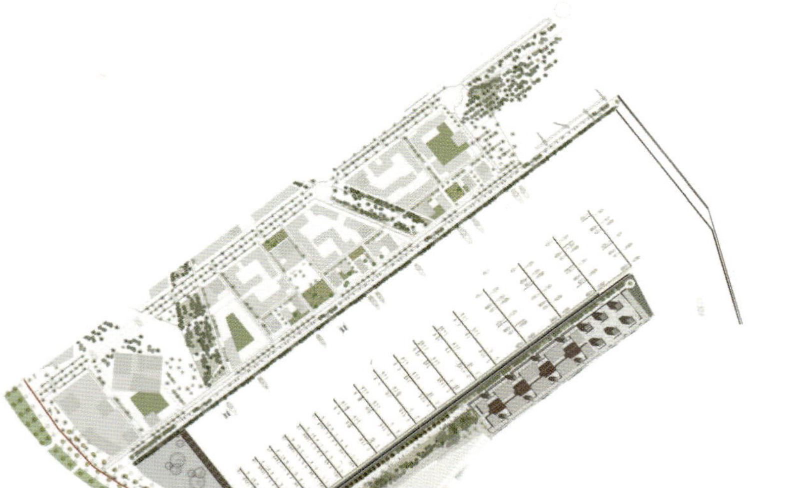

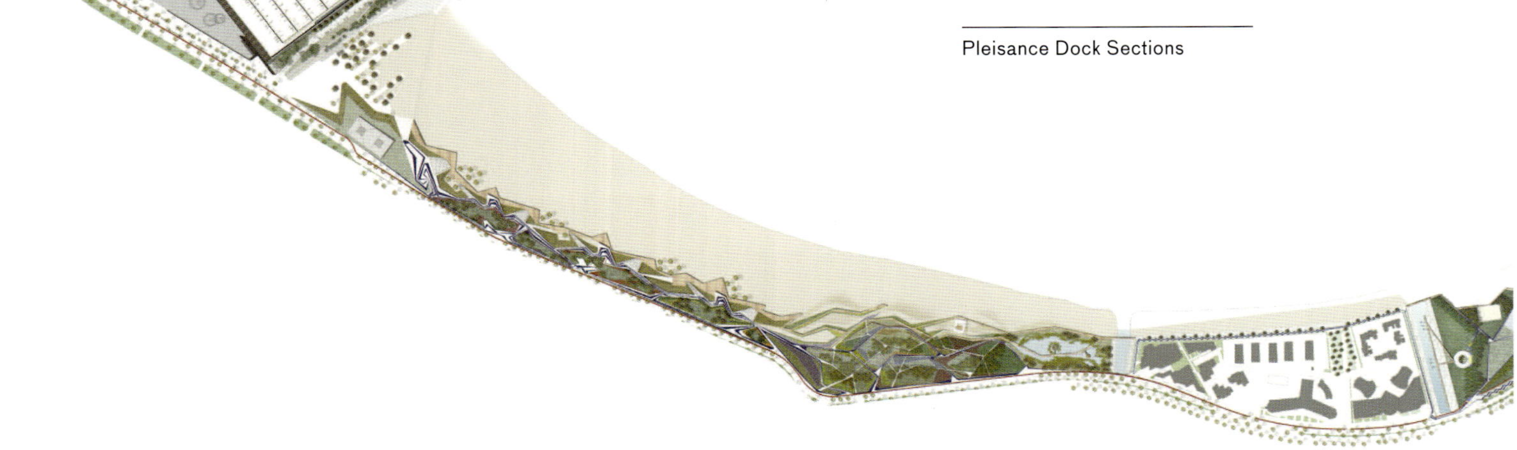

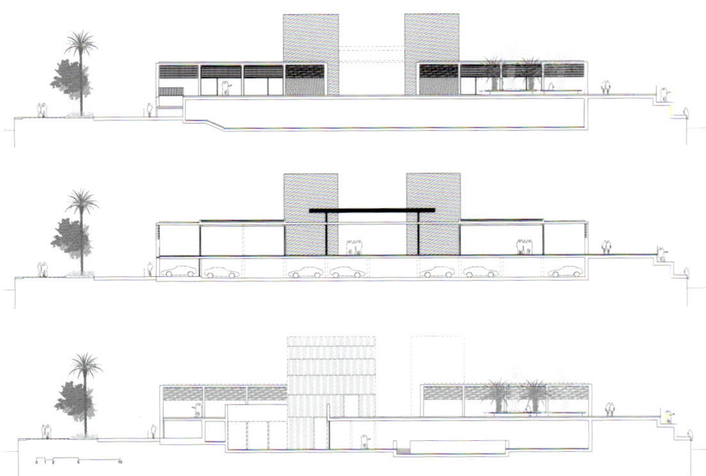

Pleisance Dock Sections

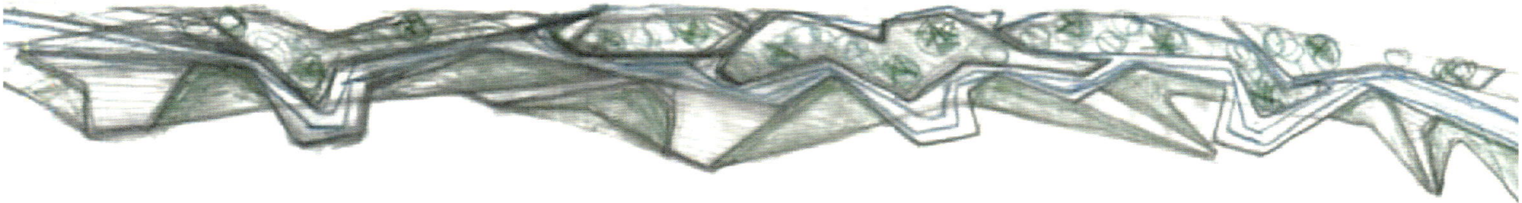

Horizonscrapers

Carlos Ferrater

The eastern side of Montjuïc facing the Ronda del Litoral and the port has a steep cliff and a profile degraded by erosion. It passes between the beautiful cemetery and the themed gardens of Costa i Llobera. You could say that it is the contrasting section or the extrados of the Botanical Garden's transept.

The actual geology of the stone of Montjuïc, its almost vertical section and coastal horizon, encouraged me to submit a design to the international competition in which Barcelona City Council requested a solution to "els cims de muntanya de Montjuïc" and to literally attach a group of buildings to the mountainside at different heights using a cantilever construction in which different activities had to be located: from a center of worship next to the cemetery, programs for city and port facilities, to horizontal structures to support the gardens as an extension of those existing in the eastern sector. The term "rascahorizontes" (horizonscrapers), known more commonly as "rascasuelos" (landscrapers), challenges the term skyscrapers, although from a structural point of view they have a similar root. Both are two cantilevered corbels subjected mainly to the lateral force of the wind as the weight of a skyscraper creates a smaller force compared to buckling due to slenderness or horizontal forces.

We had to make the most of the stone support of the mountain—as had been done in Manhattan with the granitic subsoil—in order to find structural mechanisms that made it possible for bracket structures to perform efficiently. With the help of Juan Calvo, our regular co-worker, we devised a system that would strain the upper part of the large central support beam, making it work in tension and tighten deep anchorages, while the lower section was compressed against the rock mass distributed over a large surface. A ring system distributed throughout the large central bracket helps to distribute the force, while the outer shell that forms the living areas of the building is reinforced. All the installation networks and services are located longitudinally inside this large central beam, while an exterior linear corridor is embedded and suspended in the lower section of the horizonscraper, thus resolving the escape route that continues along the emergency staircases, which are also suspended. A large column contains the lifts that ascend from the base of the mountain, acting as a strut that secures the cantilever.

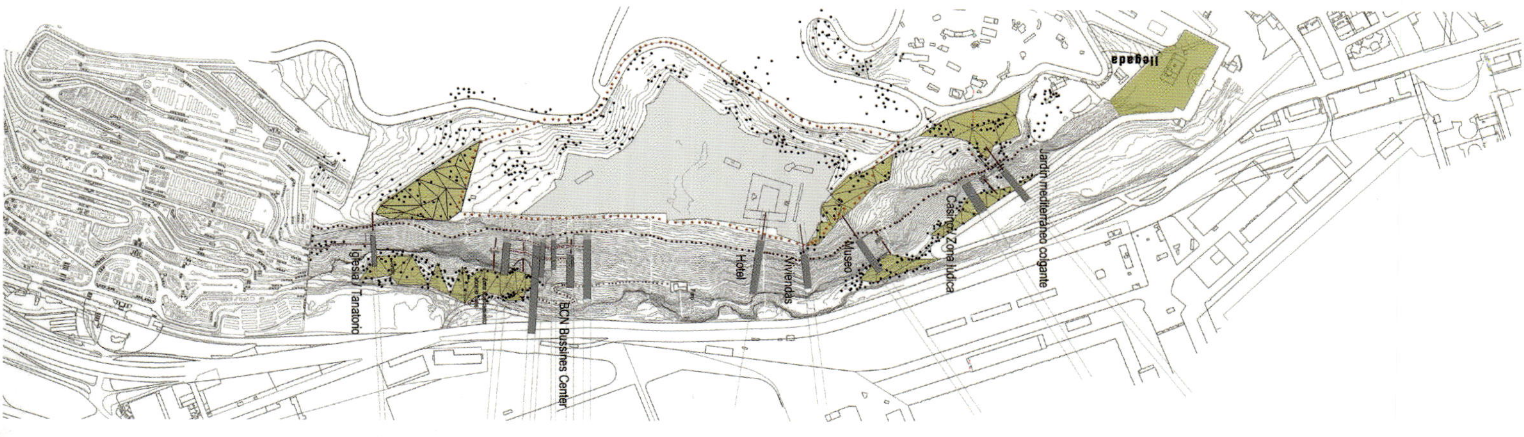

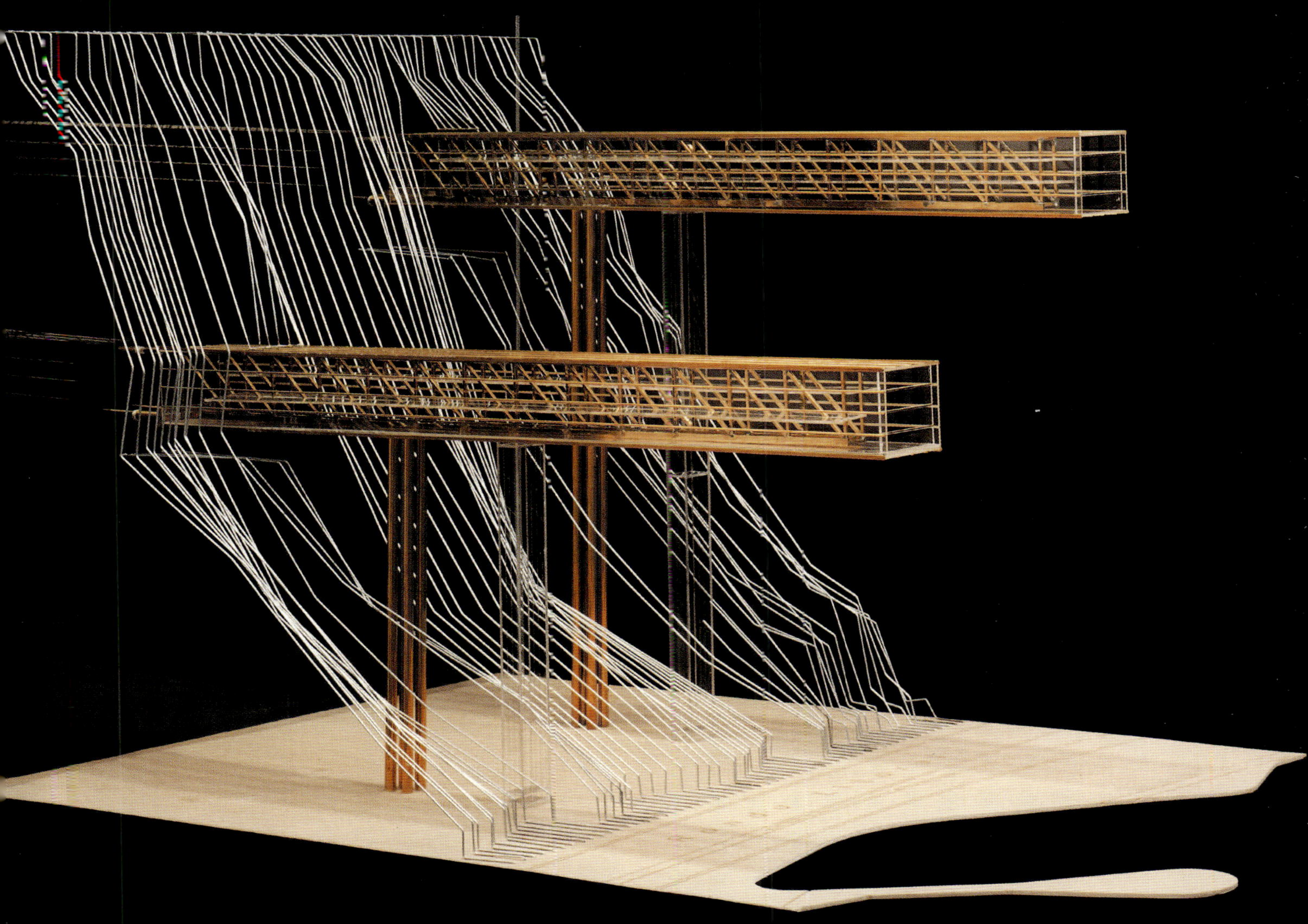

A Garden from the Sea to El Morrot: A Hinge between City and Port

Our first sketches were an exploration of diagonal lines applied onto this particular landscape: itineraries, visuals, roads, intersections, and alignments. From the beginning, the idea was to create a "park" system, capable of connecting with the unfinished sea promenade in the longitudinal direction, and with the Montjuïc hillside and the port in the transversal direction. The park was to be configured by a descending platform system connected by ramps and stairs, and viewpoints overlooking the landscape. At the same time, we studied a new project for the Ronda Litoral and for an elevated roadway over the existing viaduct. The construction must emerge from the same lines of the park, enhancing the permeability and unity of the intervention.

We intuited the hinge-like character of the area between San Bertrán Dock and the Moll de la Cost. This "hinge" space becomes a square at different levels that blends together both parts of the intervention. Our proposal is to create a seafront facade, where horizonscrapers of different lengths, up to 150 m, and variable heights, make up an area of complementary activities by the sea. This way, it provides an efficient solution to access to the castle from the base of the hill, on its most urban side. The horizonscraper becomes an entrance and a place of exchange, providing spaces for information and a great viewpoint towards the city and its port. A series of large-capacity stairs and elevators organize the accesses, overcoming a level difference equivalent to a 25-story building, simplifying the structure of the horizonscraper and providing a new entrance to the seafront side of Montjuïc. An intermediate entrance provides access at the lighthouse level via a new path.

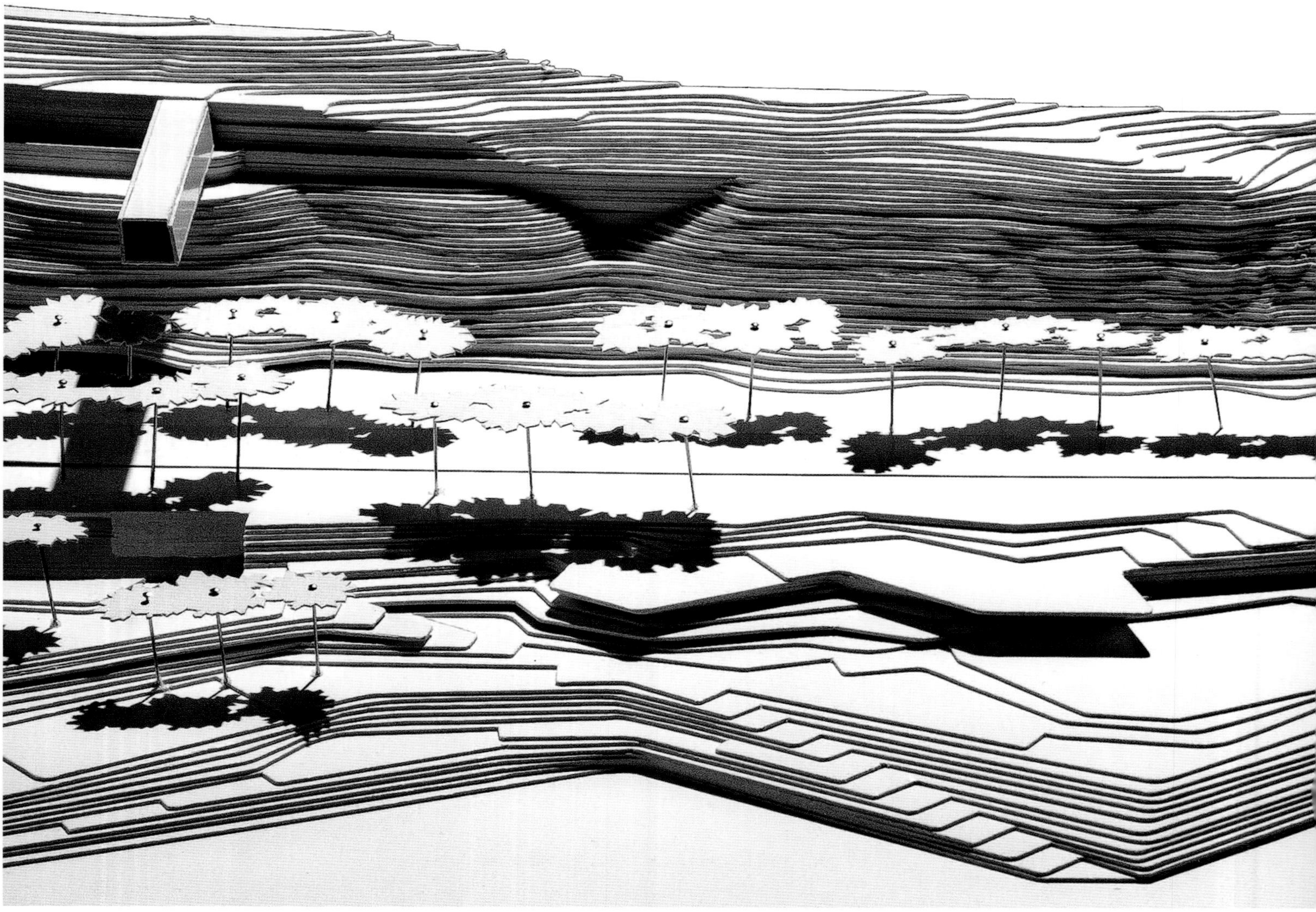

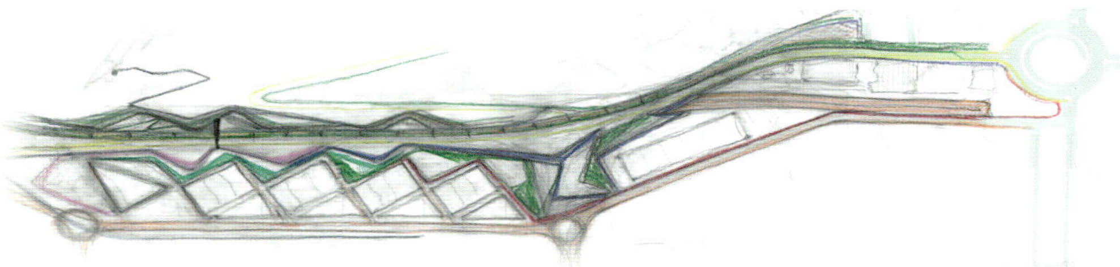

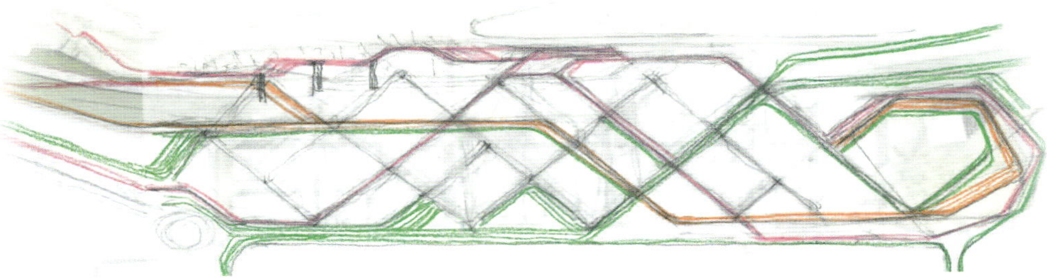

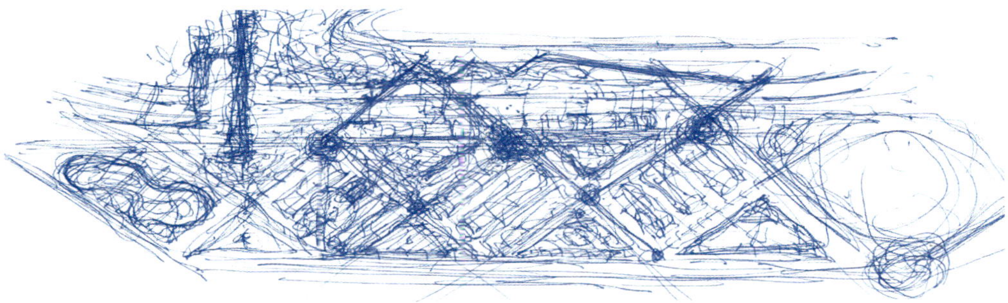

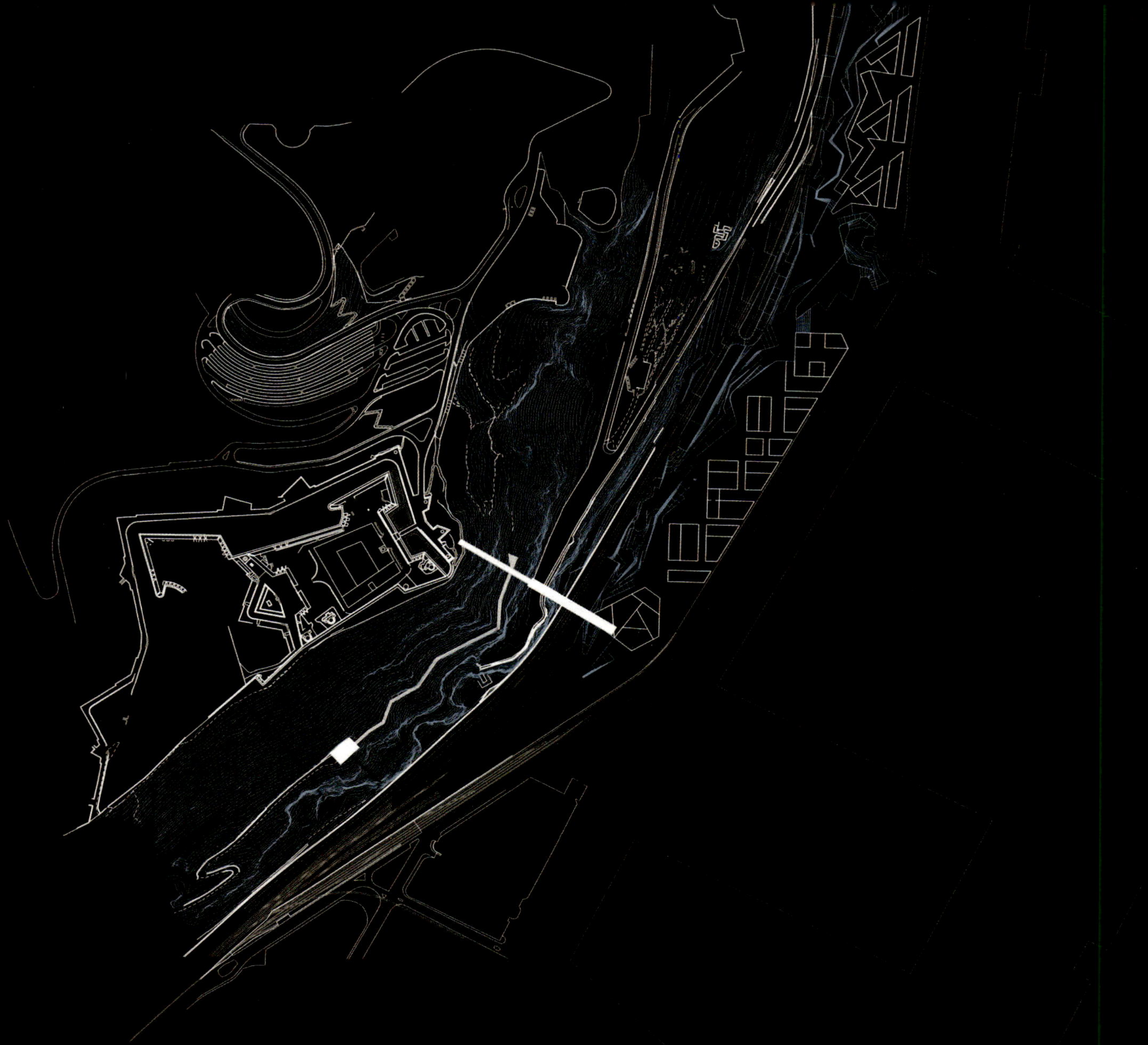

OAB

Office of Architecture in Barcelona

Carlos Ferrater Lambarri Barcelona, 1944

Doctor of Architecture and Professor of Architectural Project Design at the Polytechnic University of Catalonia. Director of the Cátedra Blanca, Barcelona.

Academician-Elect of the Real Academia de Belles Arts de Sant Jordi.

Conferred as Doctor honoris causa by the University of Trieste.

In 2006 he set up, along with Xavier Martí, Lucía Ferrater and Borja Ferrater, the Office of Architecture in Barcelona (OAB), with Núria Ayala as Projects Director.

Awarded the 2009 National Architecture Award by the Spanish Ministry of Housing for his overall career and since december 2011 member of the Royal Institute of British Architects (International RIBA Felowship).

From March 2013 he is the President of the Consell Consultiu de l'Hàbitat Urbà which is a public advisory council of the City of Barcelona .

Since 2000 he has won five FAD Prizes, the 1999 and 2008 City of Barcelona Prize, the 2005 Brunel International Architecture Award (Denmark) and the 2009 BigMat Prize. He has three times been a finalist for the Mies van der Rohe Award. He has received the City of Madrid Award, the 2001 National Spanish Architecture Award, the 2006 Dedalo Minosse International Prize in Vicenza, the 2006 Decade Award and the 2007 International Flyer Award. The 2008 RIBA International Award was given to his Editorial MP monograph, among others. He received a mention in the X Biennial of Spanish Architecture and urbanism in 2009 and in the Urban Public Space European Award 2010 for the Benidorm Waterfront which also won the FAD 2010, Saloni Awards 2010, FOPA 2009, COACV 2007-2009 Award, the Chicago Athenaeum International Architecture Award "best global design" 2010 and the CEMEX 2011. In 2011 he had also received the National Spanish Architecture Prize with the Benidorm Waterfront. He was a guest exhibitor in the International Pavilion and the Spanish Pavilion at the 2004 Venice Biennale, and was invited by the MoMA, New York, to participate in the exhibition On-Site: New Architecture in Spain, and to exhibit his work in a one-man show at the Illinois Institute of Technology's Crown Hall in Chicago, the Bilbao Fine Arts Museum, the Israel Institute of Technology, the College of Architects of Catalonia, the Foundation of the College of Architects of Madrid and the Acquario Romano. Beginning in June 2012, many models and original drawings of the Benidorm Waterfront have been chosen to form part of the collection of the Centre National d'Art et de Culture Georges Pompidou, along with the Iberia building on Paseo de Gracia and the Barcelona Botanical Garden.

Xavier Martí Galí Barcelona, 1969

Xavier Martí Galí graduated as an architect from the School of Architecture of Barcelona (ETSAB) in 1995.

He joined the Carlos Ferrater Studio as an associate architect in 2003. In 2006 he set up the Office of Architecture in Barcelona (OAB) with Carlos Ferrater, Lucía Ferrater and Borja Ferrater, with Núria Ayala as Projects Director.

He is the co-designer with Carlos Ferrater of the West Beach Promenade in Benidorm; the Mediapro Head Office on the District 22@ audiovisual Campus in Barcelona; a building on the Passeig de Gràcia; the World Trade Center Tower in Cornellà; an office building in Barcelona, the Origami House in Barcelona, the BF House in Castellón, a housing building in Bilbao and a awinery in Toro, Zamora.

He is currently working in different housing and office buildings in Barcelona and Toulouse (France) as well as the realigment of the port and waterfront of Tanger (Morocco). Other current works are a family house in Sitges (Barcelona), a Hotel in Barcelona and an office building in Guadalajara (Mexico).

He received the 2008 of City of Barcelona Prize as co-designer of the Mediapro Tower in Barcleona.

As co-designer of the Benidorm Waterfront he has received the Spanish National Architecture Award 2011, the FAD Award 2010, the WAN Award, first prize in the VIII ASCER Ceramics Awards (2009), the COACV 2007-2009 Award, the FOPA Awards 2009, the Saloni Awards 2010, the Applus Award 2010, the Chicago Athenaeum International Architecture Award "best global design" 2010, a special mention in the Urban Public Space European Award 2010. He has been finalist in Landscape European Award "Rosa Barba" and has obtained the CEMEX prize in 2011. In 2012 has received the first prize POrcelanosa "completed projects" as co-designer of the BF House in Castellón.

He has published, along with Carlos Ferrater, the books "Benidorm. West Beach Promenade" and "Carlos Ferrater & Partners" both edited by ACTAR, and the book "La Casa AA. Origami House" edited by aMag.

He has given lectures, participated in round tables and jury of prizes in Spain, China, Mexico, Italy and Estonia.

In 2012 he was invited by the Autonomous University of Barcelona (UAB) and the International University of Catalonia (UIC) as a professor. He was president of the Final Jury Reviews of the Thesis Project at La Salle University. He also has participated in Master Workshops at the UAB and the Universidad San Pablo CEU of Madrid.

Some of his works were exhibited int the Venezia Bienale in 2004 and from June 2012, many models and original drawings of the Benidorm Waterfront have been chosen to form part of the permanent collection of the Centre National d'Art et de Culture Georges Pompidou, along with the Iberia building on Passeig de Gràcia and the Barcelona Botanical Garden.

Lucía Ferrater Barcelona, 1971

Lucía Ferrater graduated as an architect from the School of Architecture of Barcelona (ETSAB) in 1997.

In 1998 she joined the Carlos Ferrater studio as an associate architect. In 2006 she helped set up the Office of Architecture in Barcelona (OAB), with Carlos Ferrater, Xavier Martí, Borja ferrater and Núria Ayala as Projects Director.

Her more important interventions in Barcelona are the refurbishing of the Coderch de Sentmenat house-studio in Plaça Calvó, a Social Services Center in the Eixample, and a housing complex in Plaça Lesseps. She has also designed an Evangelical church in Terrassa, various apartment and office buildings, two single-family houses, the Roca Barcelona Gallery, a hotel in Sitges and the Barcelona World Race Social Network. At present, she is working in the project of the Fish Market Building in Barcelona Port, a single-family house in Sitges (Barcelona), a 5* Hotel in Barcelona and several projects in the Tanger Harbor.

In 2006 she showed her Social Services Center in the Eixample of Barcelona at the MOMA, New York, in the exhibition On-Site: New Architec¬ture in Spain.

She was a finalist in the 2000 FAD Prize for Architecture with an apartment building in Sant Cugat de Vallès.

2010 Wallpaper Design Award for Roca Barcelona Gallery building.

She taught Projects of 5th and 6th-level Project Design at the International University of Catalonia's School of Architecture for three years. In 2012 she was teaching Projects in the Architectecture School of the European University of Madrid UEM. At present she is teaching Projects at the ETSAB (UPC).

Borja Ferrater Barcelona, 1978

Between 1994-1999 he conducted studies in biology at Temple University (Philadelphia, PA, USA) and at the University of Navarra (Spain).

He is a licensed architect, graduating with Thesis Cum Laude in September 2005 from the International University of Catalonia (UIC). Project Skyscraper in Athens, Greece. Visiting Student at Sciarc, Los Angeles, US Dec. 2003. Participant at "Days of Oris Symposium 2005" Zagreb, Croatia

He has taught from January to June 2006 as both fourth-year course coordinator and Design Studio teacher at the International University of Catalonia (UIC). Being guest professor in the Workshop 'Emotional City' directed by British architects Sergison & Bates (Sept. 2006).

In January 2010 he got his Masters degree in Biodigital Architecture.

Between April 2008 and September 2011 Borja was Vice-Dean of Culture Publications and International Relations at the school of Architecture, ESARQ, UIC being also director of school workshops and lectures annual program. He recently was Visiting Assistant Professor during the 2011 spring semester in Pratt Institute, New York. He currently is teaching 3rd year Studio class at ESARQ UIC.

He is author of the book "Synchronizing Geometry" published by ACTAR, which has been exhibited at the Crown Hall of the IIT (Illinois Institute of Technology), Bezalel School of Arts, Jerusalem, Instituto Cervantes in Tel Aviv, Fine Arts Museum in Bilbao, and different art galleries in Madrid and Barcelona. Recently also at the Istanbul Institute of Architects.

Founding Partner Architect of OAB (Office of Architecture in Barcelona) together with Xavier Marti, Carlos & Lucia Ferrater in January 2006.

He is a FAD (Spain's national award) prize winner in the category of "ephemeral architecture" together with Carlos Ferrater for the exhibition in Madrid: "M.C. Escher El arte de lo impossible".

Winner of Wallpaper* Design Awards 2010 for the building: Roca Barcelona Gallery together with Carlos and Lucía Ferrater. Roca Barcelona Gallery has also been finalist of the Lamp awards 2010 in the category of Interior lightning, and has received a special citation at 2010 IALD International Lighting Design Awards , Las Vegas, NV USA, May 2010. Recently, In may 2011 Borja also won the "Good Design is Good Business" awards organized by Architectural Record magazine with the RBG building.

He has given lectures, participated in round tables and jury of prizes in Sweden, Norway, Germany, USA, Israel, UK, Japan, Turkey, Italy, Romania, and Spain. He has also had articles published about many of his works in multiple magazines, catalogues, and other publications.

Núria Ayala Prats Barcelona, 1975

Núria Ayala graduated as an architect from the School of Architecture of Barcelona (ETSAB) in 2001.

She joined the Carlos Ferrater studio in 2000.

She is the Projects Director, collaborator and co-author of different works, projects and competitions, including the NGO "Centre Esplai" (hostel, training facilities, offices and fitness center); the Musée des Confluences in Lyon; Casa Nolla; the GISA and FGC institutional Headquarters on Via Augusta in Barcelona; Las Palmas de Gran Canaria Promenade; the hotel in the Almodovar Gate in Cordoba; the Azahar Business Group Headquarters in Castellón; the new City Hall in Palma de Mallorca; the new IMQ Hospital in Bilbao; the development plan for the Garellano area of Bilbao; the La Seda Head Office in Barcelona; the City of Music in Sabadell; the extension to the Barcelona Botanical garden; the project design for Barcelona High Court; the extension to Torreblanca Park, Summer Camp NGO Viladoms, Club House in Bodrum – Turkey and Mixed use Buildings in the Miami Design Disctrict .

Together with Carlos Ferrater she received, on 2010, Ibeoramerican Biennial Architectural Prize, Ecola Prize and Finalist in Valencian Award for Azahar Business Group Headquarters. On 2011, Finalist in the XI Spanish Biennial and Finalist in FAD Prize for Summer Camp NGO Viladoms.

She coordinated and did the graphic design for the "Research Process" in Sincronizar la geometría/ Synchronizing Geometry, published by Actar; Editorial MP's monograph Carlos Ferrater - OAB, the book "Casas y habitants" (Actar) and Actar's monograph "OAB. Office of Architecture in Barcelona"

Alberto Peñín Llobell, 1970

Architect

Architect from ETSA Valencia in 1995 when he joined Peñín Architects, established in Valencia and Barcelona with special attention to urban and territorial design and, rehabilitation, housing and public buildings.

His practice has been awarded with first price in around fifteen professional competitions. His work, in buildings as "Centro del Imserso" or "Aula Magna de Gandía" has been selected at Young Architects of Spain, awarded at several occasions among which Valencia Order of Architects and Spanish and Latin American Bienal, and published at several professional magazines as TC monograph "Peñín Arquitectos", Arquitectura Viva, ViA, or AMC. AXA Association member from 2011.

Regular partner of Carlos Ferrater since 1997 and associated office of OAB since its creation in many works and projects in Spain, France, and Turkey. Among many projects and competitions made with OAB, he also built "Offices at Boulogne", "Vila-real library", "Social houses"at Torrent and Castellón, and the work in progress "Union of Lawyers headquarters and offices" at Lyon and two housing projects in Toulouse, France.

European PhD from UPC (2007) Design Professor at ETSAB school of architecture of Barcelona since 1999 where he is currently vice dean. He is director with Carlos Ferrater of the Barcelona White Chair and of the magazine and publisher house Palimpsesto. With an extensive academic life as lecturer, design professor or master's teacher, he has participated in seminars, workshops or final diploma jurys in Cooper Union (NY) and schools of architecture in Paris, Venice, Berlin, Monterrey, Milano, Madrid or Valencia.

CREDITS

BALMES 145 BUILDING

LOCATION BALMES 145. BARCELONA
DATE PROJECT 2000 – REALIZATION 2002
ARCHITECT OAB. CARLOS FERRATER
PHOTO A.BAGUÉ - J. GUILLAMAT

BARCELONA BOTANICAL GARDEN BOTANICAL INSTITUTE BUILDING - CSIC

LOCATION MONTJUÏC MOUNTAIN, BARCELONA
PROMOTER AJUNTAMENT DE BARCELONA
DATE PROJECT: 1995 REALIZATION: 1998-1999 (JBB)
PROJECT: 2000 REALIZATION: 2001-2003 (CSIC)
PROJECT: 2007 REALIZATION: 2007-2008 (EXTENSION)
ARCHITECT OAB. CARLOS FERRATER
WITH J.L. CANOSA & BET FIGUERAS (PROJECT)
WITH JOAN GUIBERNAU – CSIC
WITH NÚRIA AYALA - EXTENSION 2007
WITH NÚRIA AYALA - MAINTENANCE BUILDING 2015
PHOTO A. BAGUE - AERIAL TAVISA - J. GUILLAMAT (PHOTO 2012)

VERTIX DIAGONAL BUILDING

LOCATION CRISTOFOL DE MOURA ST / BAC DE RODA ST. BARCELONA
DATE PROJECT: 2003 - REALIZATION: 2007
ARCHITECT OAB. C. FERRATER - X. MARTI / C.PUEYO
PHOTO A.BAGUÉ - J. GUILLAMAT (PHOTO 2013)

M-3 LESSEPS BUILDING

LOCATION VELÁZQUEZ ST, RIERA DE VALLCARCA ST, BARCELONA
DATES PROJECT: 2004 - REALIZATION: 2008
ARCHITECT OAB. CARLOS FERRATER - LUCIA FERRATER - XAVIER MARTÍ
PHOTO A. BAGUÉ - J. GUILLAMAT (PHOTO 2012)

INTERMODAL STATION "ZARAGOZA-DELICIAS"

LOCATION ZARAGOZA
DATE PROJECT: 1999 - REALIZATION: 2001-2003
ARCHITECT OAB.CARLOS FERRATER / JOSE M. VALERO WITH FELIX ARRANZ – ELENA MATEU
STRUCTURE JUAN CALVO. PONDIO
PHOTO A.BAGUÉ

INTERMODAL BUILDING OF BARCELONA AIRPORT

LOCATION AEROPUERTO DE EL PRAT. BARCELONA
DATE PROJECT: 2002 - REALIZATION: 2007
ARCHITECT OAB. C. FERRATER / R. SANABRIA – J.M. CASADEVALL
PHOTO A.BAGUÉ

MURCIA AIRPORT

LOCATION MURCIA
DATE PROJECT: 2009 - REALIZATION: 2010-2012
ARCHITECT OAB. C. FERRATER / R. SANABRIA – J.M. CASADEVALL
PHOTO A.BAGUÉ

MULTIHOUSING BUILDING IN BARCELONA

LOCATION PASSEIG DE GRÀCIA, 23 - DIPUTACIÓ, 259
DATE PROJECT: 1996 - REALIZATION: 1999
ARCHITECT OAB. CARLOS FERRATER / JOAN GUIBERNAU WITH XAVIER MARTÍ GALÍ
PHOTO J.M. MOLINOS

MULTIHOUSING BUILDING IN BARCELONA

LOCATION PASSEIG DE GRÀCIA, 99
DATE PROJECT: 2004 - REALIZATION: 2005-2007
ARCHITECT OAB. CARLOS FERRATER - LUCÍA FERRATER WITH JOAN GUIBERNAU & ELENA MATEU
PHOTO A.BAGUÉ - J. GUILLAMAT (PHOTO 2013)

HOTEL MANDARIN IN BARCELONA

LOCATION PASSEIG DE GRÀCIA, 38-40
DATE PROJECT: 2007 – REALIZATION: 2010
ARCHITECT OAB. CARLOS FERRATER / JUAN TRIAS DE BES
INTERIOR DESIGN PATRICIA URQUIOLA / GCA
PHOTO D. ROVIRA - J. GUILLAMAT (PHOTO 2013)

SCIENCE PARK IN GRANADA

LOCATION AV. DEL MEDITERRANEO S/N
DATE PROJECT: 2004 - REALIZATION: 2005-2008
ARCHITECT OAB. C.FERRATER / E. JIMENEZ -Y. BRASA
STRUCTURE JUAN CALVO. PONDIO
PHOTO A.BAGUÉ - J. GUILLAMAT (PHOTO 2015)

MULTIHOUSING BUILDING IN BILBAO

LOCATION EUSKADI SQ, BILBAO
DATE PROJECT: 2005 – REALIZATION: 2007-2011
ARCHITECT OAB. C. FERRATER - X. MARTÍ - L. FERRATER / L. DOMÍNGUEZ
STRUCTURE IDOM
PHOTO J. GUILLAMAT

IMQ HOSPITAL IN BILBAO

LOCATION DEUSTO, BILBAO
DATE PROJECT: 2009 – REALIZATION: 2010-2012
ARCHITECT OAB. CARLOS FERRATER / ALFONSO CASARES WITH NÚRIA AYALA / A. OCAÑA / L. DOMÍNGUEZ
STRUCTURE JUAN CALVO. PONDIO
PHOTO J. GUILLAMAT

AQU LEIA TOWER

LOCATION JESOLO, VENECIA, ITALIA
DATE PROJECT: 2004 – REALIZATION: 2009
ARCHITECT OAB. CARLOS FERRATER / GUSTAVO CARABAJAL WITH XAVIER MARTÍ GALÍ
STRUCTURE MASSIMO MAJOWIECKI
PHOTO A. CHEMOLLO, F. ORSENIGO

NGO VILADOMS / NGO CENTRE ESPLAI

LOCATION CTRA BV-1212 KM.5,15 – CASTELLBELL I EL VILAR
DATE PROJECT: 2010 – REALIZATION: 2010
ARCHITECT OAB. CARLOS FERRATER - NÚRIA AYALA
PHOTO A. BAGUÉ

THE AZAHAR GROUP HEADQUARTERS

LOCATION CARRETERA NACIONAL 340 . CASTELLÓN
DATE PROJECT: 2004 - REALIZATION: 2009
ARCHITECT OAB. CARLOS FERRATER - NÚRIA AYALA
PHOTO A. BAGUÉ

ALENTI HOTEL

LOCATION INDUSTRIA SQ.- 1º DE MAYO ST. SITGES
DATE PROJECT: 2007 - REALIZATION: 2009
ARCHITECT OAB. CARLOS FERRATER - LUCÍA FERRATER
PHOTO L. CASALS - J. RODRÍGUEZ

UNITED EVANGELICA CHURCH IN BARCELONA

LOCATION BÉJAR AV. TERRASSA
DATE PROJECT: 2007 - REALIZATION: 2008-2010
ARCHITECT OAB. CARLOS FERRATER - LUCÍA FERRATER
PHOTO A. BAGUÉ - J. GUILLAMAT (PHOTO 2014)

MICHELIN HEADQUARTERS BUILDING

LOCATION ZAC SEGUIN RIVES DE SEINE - BOULOGNE
DATE PROJECT: 2007 - REALIZATION: 2010
ARCHITECTS OAB. C. FERRATER / E.BABIN - F. RENAUD - A.PEÑIN
PHOTO D. ROVIRA – J. GUILLAMAT (PHOTO 2012)

MEDIAPRO BUILDING

LOCATION DIAGONAL AV. 177-183, 22@ DISTRICT, BCN
DATE PROJECT: 2005 - REALIZATION: 2008
ARCHITECT OAB. CARLOS FERRATER / PATRICK GENARD WITH XAVIER MARTI GALÍ
STRUCTURE JUAN CALVO. PONDIO
PHOTO A. BAGUE - J. GUILLAMAT (PHOTO 2012)

CORPORATE HEADQUARTERS FOR GISA AND FGC

LOCATION VIA AUGUSTA - VERGOS ST. BARCELONA
DATE PROJECT: 2006 - REALIZATION 2009
ARCHITECT OAB. CARLOS FERRATER - NÚRIA AYALA
PHOTO A. BAGUÉ

ROCA BARCELONA GALLERY

LOCATION JOAN GÜELL, 211. BARCELONA
DATE PROJECT: 2008 - REALIZATION: 2009
ARCHITECT OAB. B.FERRATER - C. FERRATER - L. FERRATER
STRUCTURE JORDI BERNUZ
PHOTO A. BAGUÉ

BENIDORM WEST BEACH PROMENADE

LOCATION BENIDORM. ALICANTE
DATE COMPETITION: 2002 - REALIZATION: 2006-2009
ARCHITECT OAB. CARLOS FERRATER - XAVIER MARTÍ GALÍ
STRUCTURE JUAN CALVO. PONDIO
PHOTO A. BAGUÉ - J. GUILLAMAT (PHOTO 2014)

108 SOCIAL HOUSING

LOCATION JOSEP TARRADELLAS Av. - L'HOSPITALET. BCN
DATE PROJECT: 2012 - REALIZATION: 2013-2014
ARCHITECT OAB. CARLOS FERRATER - NÚRIA AYALA WITH CC245. SERGI BLANCH - SANDRA RODÀ
PHOTO J. GUILLAMAT

VILA REAL PUBLIC LIBRARY

LOCATION VILA REAL, CASTELLON
DATE PROJECT: 2009 - REALIZATION: 2009 - 2011
ARCHITECT OAB. C. FERRATER / A. PEÑIN WITH J. GIMENO
PHOTO A. BAGUÉ

HOUSE IN ALCANAR

LOCATION LES CASES D'ALCANAR. TARRAGONA
DATE PROJECT: 2003 - REALIZATION: 2006
ARCHITECT OAB. CARLOS FERRATER WITH CARLOS ESCURA
PHOTO A. BAGUÉ

AA HOUSE - ORIGAMI

LOCATION BARCELONA
DATE 2007 - 2009
ARCHITECT OAB CARLOS FERRATER - XAVIER MARTÍ
STRUCTURE JUAN CALVO. PONDIO
PHOTO A. BAGUÉ - J. RODRÍGUEZ

BF HOUSE

LOCATION URB. LA COMA. BORRIOL. CASTELLÓN
DATE PROJECT: 2006 - REALIZATION: 2011
ARCHITECT OAB. CARLOS FERRATER - XAVIER MARTÍ GALÍ ADI. CARLOS ESCURA - CARLOS MARTIN
PHOTO J. GUILLAMAT

REFURBISHMENT OF PARENT'S HOUSE IN L'ESCALA

LOCATION L'ESCALA. GIRONA
DATE PROJECT: 2012 - REALIZATION: 2013
ARCHITECT OAB. CARLOS FERRATER WITH GERARD OLIVÉ (REALIZATION)
PHOTO A. BAGUÉ

CLUSTER KAPLANKAYA IN BODRUM

LOCATION BODRUM. TURKEY
DATE PROJECT: 2011 - REALIZATION: 2012-2013
ARCHITECT OAB. CARLOS FERRATER - BORJA FERRATER
PHOTO J. GUILLAMAT

IN PROGRESS

LAW SOCIETY IN LYON

LOCATION LYON. FRANCE
DATE COMPETITION: 2015
ARCHITECT OAB. C. FERRATER / A. PEÑIN / B. DUMETIER

CAMBÓ AVENUE HOTEL IN BARCELONA

LOCATION AVDA. CAMBÓ. BARCELONA
DATE PROJECT: 2014
ARCHITECT OAB. CARLOS FERRATER - XAVIER MARTÍ GALÍ

CANYON RANCH HOTEL IN BODRUM

LOCATION BODRUM. TURKEY
DATE PROJECT: 2011 - REALIZATION: 2012-2013
ARCHITECT OAB. C.FERRATER - B. FERRATER / J. TRIAS DE BES
INTERIOR DESIGN GCA
PHOTO J. GUILLAMAT

TOWER IN GUADALAJARA. MEXICO

LOCATION AVDA. PATRIA. GUADALAJARA. MEXICO
DATE PROJECT: 2013 - REALIZATION: 2015
ARCHITECT OAB. CARLOS FERRATER - XAVIER MARTÍ GALÍ

CORNICHE OF TANGIER / PORT OF TANGIER

LOCATION TANGIER. MOROCCO
DATE PROJECT: 2013
ARCHITECT OAB. CARLOS FERRATER - XAVIER MARTÍ GALÍ OAB. CARLOS FERRATER - LUCÍA FERRATER

MIXED USE BUILDING IN MIAMI. USA

LOCATION MIAMI DESIGN DISTRICT. MIAMI USA
DATE PROJECT: 2012-2013
ARCHITECT OAB. CARLOS FERRATER - BORJA FERRATER

NITERÓ BEACH PROMENADE

LOCATION BAHÍA DE RIO DE JANEIRO. BRASIL
DATE PROJECT: 2013
ARCHITECT OAB. CARLOS FERRATER

THE FISH MARKET IN BARCELONA'S PORT

LOCATION BARCELONA'S PORT
DATE PROJECT: 2015
ARCHITECT OAB. C. FERRATER - L. FERRATER / J. COLL

"HORIZONSCRAPER" IN THE SEAFRONT OF BARCELONA

LOCATION BARCELONA'S WATERFRONT
DATE PROJECT: 2014
ARCHITECT OAB. CARLOS FERRATER
PHOTO A. BAGUÉ

A GARDEN FROM THE SEA TO THE MORROT

LOCATION BARCELONA'S WATERFRONT
DATE PROJECT: 2015
ARCHITECT OAB. CARLOS FERRATER - XAVIER MARTÍ GALÍ
PHOTO J. GUILLAMAT

Carlos Ferrater Projects 1970-2005

The career of Carlos Ferrater (1944) got under way in the context of a an outdated modernism. His first piece of work, 54 dwellings in the Sant Just Park housing complex in Sant Just Desvern, was rooted in the oeuvre of José Antonio Coderch: it announced a recurrent wish for realism, for efficiency, for tempered rationalism adapted to the context. The apartment buildings in Barcelona's Carrer Bertrán were a demonstration of his ability to progress in terms of typological invention. These early buildings, with their abstraction and transparency, could be brought into line with Mediterranean classicism. This same period witnessed his recourse to the lightness of pavilions in which mass dematerialized, the inspiration being the architecture of Mies van der Rohe, as shown by the sports pavilion in Torroella de Montgrí. And that first phase culminated in the Guix de la Meda house, the Garbí building and the design for the Yacht Club in L'Estartit.

The boom prior to the Olympic Games was a busy time for Ferrater, as his team took on a number of projects that were highly representative of Olympic Barcelona: the three city blocks in the Olympic Village, the dwellings in Vall d'Hebron, the Hotel Juan Carlos I (1988-92), and the Botanical Garden, the competition for which he won in 1989. This volumetric forcefulness led to the creation of almost intimate open spaces within the city block, thus endowing public space. Following the Olympic period, the possibility arose for new experiments like the "minimalism" of the IMPIVA in Castellón, and the introduction of fractal forms, first developed in the Fitness Center for the Hotel Juan Carlos I. Ferrater's team carried out two further experiments: the studio-house for a photographer in Llampaies, and the Arruga Film Studios in Sant Just Desvern. And the period concluded with the Convention Center on the Diagonal.

Prior to the creation in 2005 of OAB (Office of Architecture in Barcelona), some of the practice's most representative buildings were completed, including such highly regarded works as the block in Carrer Roger de Flor, the Ibiza house, the new El Prat Royal Golf Club, and the International JC Decaux Headquarters. This period culminated with the Castelln Auditorium Center.

Text by Josep Maria Montaner, historian and Professor of Composition at the Architecture School of Barcelona, ETSAB (UPC).

Photo: J.M. Ferrater

Instant City 1971

Photo: C. Ferrater

Sant Just Park 1973 - 1976

Photo: L. Casals

Bertran 67 Multihousing building 1981-1982

Photo: L. Casals

Sports Pavillion in Torroella de Montgrí. Girona 1988

Photo: L. Casals

Garbí Building in L' Estartit. Girona 1986-1988

Photo: L. Casals

Guix de la Meda House. L' Estartit. Girona 1983

Photo: J. Guillamat

Yatch Club in L'Estartit. Girona 1991-1993

Photo: A. Bagué

Botanical Garden in Barcelona. 1989-2015

Photo: L. Casals

Rey Juan Carlos I Hotel 1992

Photo: J. Guillamat

Olympic Village in Poblenou. Barcelona 1992

Photo: J. Guillamat

Olympic Village in Valle Hebron. Barcelona 1992

Photo: A. Bagué

Catalonia Convention Center 2000

Photo: L. Casals

Technological Park IMPIVA 1995

Photo: L. Casals

House-studio in Llampaies 1995

Photo: L. Casals

Fitness Center 1996

Photo: L. Casals

Arruga Movie Studio 1997

Photo: L. Casals

Triginer house 1996

Photo: L. Casals

Guest Pavillion in Menorca 1995

Photo: A. Bagué

Tagomago House in Eivissa 2001

Photo: A. Bagué

El Prat Royal Golf Club 2004

Photo: A. Bagué

International JC Decaux Headquarters 2001

Photo: A. Bagué

Social Services Center in Roger de Flor's Block 2003

Photo: A. Bagué

Castellón Convention Center 2004